CONTENTS

||||||||||||||||||||||||||||||||||||||||||||||||||||

W9-BDO-855

ACKNOWLEDGMENTS

||||||||||||||||||||||||||||||||||||||||||||||||||||||||||||||||||||||||||||||||||||

I VIVIDLY REMEMBER the day we had our first son. Labor pains started in the early morning—and despite the doctor's advice to wait until the contractions were fairly close together—we wimped out and headed for the hospital.

Nine hours later, a huge head finally emerged, inspiring me to exclaim, "It's a boy!" (I had no idea if I was right, but something that big *had* to belong to a boy.) I was right. The vitals were checked. The baby was cleaned, prepped, swaddled, and then dropped in his mother's lap. He was now officially "ours." Yet, in spite of the enormity of months of worrying, birthing classes, crib shopping, baby name books, room painting, waiting, waiting, and more waiting—culminating in several hours of sheer terror and excitement during the birthing process—I thought out loud, "Well, this wasn't so bad! Let's have another." And so we did, and then again.

And with each one came the realization that they actually needed to be *taught* something. In fact, many things. Many, many things. When my oldest was close to six—and his younger brother about four—I took them to a bowling alley. As we entered the lanes, the sounds and sights took hold of them. "What in the world *is* this place?" they wondered. Their senses were overwhelmed, and they were *captivated*. I caught their wide-eyed expressions and laughed—and then it dawned on me. They were like little aliens visiting this planet for the first time—and *I* was their guide, their compass, their teacher. Yes, *everything* was new to them, and everything had to be taught to them. And just when you got through educating the first one about something, darned if the second one didn't need to hear the same things again and again. After a while (probably out of desperation!), I started to compose a lengthy list of things they needed to know. I even devised a learning game for the boys—asking them questions about important topics on car trips, then watching all three minds scramble for the right answer. Right or wrong, they embraced the fun of the competition—and the goal of "learning something" became fulfilled.

Clearly, without the inclusion of their inquisitive minds in my life, there simply wouldn't be a *Man Test*. So, it is with great pleasure that I acknowledge my boys—Conner, Brett, and Alex—as the sole inspiration for this book.

INTRODUCTION

||||||||||||||||||||||||||||||||||||||||||||||||||||||||||||||||||||||

WHY IS IT that some men succeed while others do not? Why do certain men seem to breeze through life while others constantly struggle? The answer can largely be found in one concept: *preparation.* Only a few generations ago, it would have been unheard of to send a boy out on his own without a comprehensive education about shelter, food, clothing, his livelihood, and general life skills. He knew how to build a home, and chances are he had already helped his dad to build and/or repair his own home. Food was grown within yards of the front door, and a boy knew exactly how and when to plant—and then harvest—his dinner. Meat, milk, and hides for clothing were a few steps away in the barn. If need be, a boy studied a skill as an apprentice, insuring competency for an income-producing occupation. Yes, life *was* simpler then, and preparation for manhood was fairly straightforward and uncomplicated.

In today's complex society, we're now confronted with thousands of difficult decisions and choices on a daily basis. Which one of the hundreds of career paths should I follow? Should I rent or buy a home? How do I put out this grease fire? Where should I invest my money? How can I get the best price for this car? Will they allow this through airport security? How we *respond* to these challenges determines our ultimate success. The more prepared we are, the better our chances of succeeding. Conversely, a lack of preparation may lead to an unfulfilled life of frustration and disappointments. Preparation comes from knowledge, and without the knowledge, we simply resort to guessing—often with disastrous results.

But where's an outline, a list, or a "manual" to guide you on the thousands of things that you absolutely have to learn? Well, until now there wasn't one—making the task of becoming an independent, self-confident young man even more difficult. This is the sole motivation behind *The Man Test*—an essential and comprehensive guide containing the information every man should learn and master.

Each topic in *The Man Test* begins with a challenging quiz about each subject. Test your knowledge in each subject and then compare your answers to the answer key. If you know the answers, simply move on to the next topic, or refresh your memory by reading the answers and explanations given for some of the more difficult questions. You're also encouraged to explore further web-based and published resources to expand your knowledge in the selected topic.

To simplify all there is to learn, *The Man Test* is divided into nine chapters representing the following life-critical categories:

- Manners and Etiquette
- Career and Employment
- Home Renting and Buying
- Finance and Negotiation

- Transportation
- Urban and Outdoor Survival
- Domestic Skills
- Home Maintenance
- Health, Nutrition, and Lifestyle

HOW TO READ *THE MAN TEST*

This book exists to give you a broad-based wealth of knowledge in the nine life-critical categories. You may simply want to sit down and start testing yourself from the beginning. You may also want to skip around to topics in which you need the most help. Keep this book handy as an ongoing guide and reference for when you're faced with interesting life challenges.

By the end of this book, you should be informed, entertained, and well on your way to becoming a self-confident, capable, and "complete" man.

MANNERS AND ETIQUETTE

WHO NEEDS GOOD manners? Well, for one, you do. Your ability to get ahead in life may be largely contingent upon the impression you make on others. Good impressions tend to open up opportunities that can help you succeed. Conversely, making a poor impression will likely alienate many people who could otherwise benefit you.

What about dating? In spite of what we want to believe, there are very specific rules that you'll need to know if you want to get to the *second* date. This section will help you discover if you're ready to make a great impression in both your personal and business lives. You'll also learn how to elevate what others think about you.

1

TELEPHONE AND TEXTING

There was a time when nails were high-tech. There was a time when people had to be told how to use a telephone. Technology is just a tool. People use tools to improve their lives.

—TOM CLANCY, AUTHOR

1. What percentage of people agreed they'd be more likely to accept a first date if they were "texted" first?
   a. 0%—texting is too impersonal and tends to ruin any chance for a date
   b. 7%
   c. 26%
   d. 79%
   e. 91%

2. (True/False) You got a call from a number you didn't recognize and no message was left on your voice mail. It's okay to call the person back.

3. According to conventional etiquette, what are the earliest and latest times that it's appropriate to call someone?
   a. 7:00 a.m., 9:00 p.m.
   b. 8:00 a.m., 10:00 p.m.
   c. 9:00 a.m., 9:30 p.m.

4. What percentage of driving accidents involves talking on a cell phone and/or texting?
   a. 2%
   b. 6%
   c. 11%
   d. 21%
   e. 28%

5. A friend calls you, but you get disconnected during the call. Who should call back? You, or the person who placed the call?
   a. You call back
   b. The person who called you

6. (True/False) It's appropriate to use a cell phone in a social environment as long as the call is business-related.

7. When is it appropriate to use a speakerphone?

   a. Never

   b. Only with close friends

   c. Only after you ask permission

8. A call is coming into your phone, and the caller ID identifies the person. What is the proper etiquette when greeting the caller?

   a. Do not use the caller's name before he identifies himself.

   b. Immediately let him know you know who's calling.

THE ANSWER KEY

1. *c.* 26%

A survey by AT&T also revealed this about texters:

- 40% of people in a relationship believe that texting plays a major role.
- About one-third would feel more comfortable to get a text prior to their first date.
- One-quarter have updated friends and relatives during their blind dates.
- 6% have broken up with a text message!

2. False

This is usually only appropriate when someone leaves a message requesting that you call back. If you call someone back based solely on his caller ID, you might sound stupid, or worse yet—desperate (not the impression you want to leave with a girl!).

3. *c.* 9:00 a.m., 9:30 p.m.

4. *e.* 28%

Every year 1.4 million car crashes involve cell phones, and 200,000 are caused by texting.

5. *b.* The person who called you

6. False

Using a cell phone in a social environment has become almost akin to sneezing without covering your face! If you have to use the phone, excuse yourself and find a more suitable location.

7. *c*. Only after you ask permission

8. *a*. Do not use the caller's name before he identifies himself.

If the caller is a close friend, then you can let him know right away that you know who is calling.

TABLE MANNERS

The children now love luxury; they have bad manners, contempt for authority; they show disrespect for elders and love chatter in place of exercise. Children are now tyrants, not the servants of their households. They no longer rise when elders enter the room. They contradict their parents, chatter before company, gobble up dainties at the table, cross their legs, and tyrannize their teachers.

— SOCRATES, C. 469 BC–399 BC

1. (True/False) You put something in your mouth that's inedible, e.g., a bone fragment or a piece of gristle. It's okay to "spit it out" into your napkin.

2. (True/False) You just took a big bite of food, and someone asks you a question. It's okay to respond even though you have food in your mouth.

3. (True/False) Toothpicks are available at the counter in a restaurant. It's not acceptable to use one publicly after you finish eating.

4. (True/False) By request, you're passing something at the table. It's all right to help yourself to a portion "on the way" as long as there's an ample amount for both of you.

5. When is it appropriate to begin eating after being served?
   a. The minute the food is placed in front of you
   b. When the host picks up his or her fork to begin eating
   c. When other guests at the table begin to eat

6. After you've finished your meal, where should you place your napkin?
   a. On the table in front of you
   b. On your chair
   c. On the table to the left of your plate

7. Someone passed you the bread basket and you chose a piece. Where do you put it, and how do you prepare it for eating?
   a. On your dinner plate, then butter it whole
   b. On the small plate to your left, then butter it whole
   c. On the small plate to your left, then break off a bite-sized piece and butter it
   d. On the table in front of you, then break it in half before buttering

8. You just finished eating. Where and how do you leave your cutlery?

    a. In the middle of your dinner plate, fork pointing down, knife alongside

    b. In their original positions, placed directly on the table

    c. On the right side of your plate, fork up, knife alongside

    d. On the small plate to your left, fork pointing up, knife alongside

9. You're sitting down for a seven-course dinner. How do you know which silverware to use for each course?

    a. Start with the utensils farthest out from your plate and work your way in with each course.

    b. Start with the utensils closest to your plate and work your way out with each course.

    c. There is no set rule.

10. You're leaving the table, but are not yet finished with your meal. What should you do with your silverware to indicate to the hostess/waiter that you're still eating?

    a. Place your silverware back in its original position.

    b. Place all silverware on the bread plate to your left.

c. Place your silverware on your dinner plate, fork, spoon, and knife resting normally.

d. Place your silverware to the right of your dinner plate, fork, spoon, and knife resting normally.

e. Take your silverware with you to the restroom.

THE ANSWER KEY

1. False

No spitting! Instead, calmly bring the napkin to your mouth and then push the inedible item into the cloth with your tongue. You can also inconspicuously remove the offending object with your fingers and then place it in the napkin.

2. False

This is never appropriate. Even if you've taken a big bite at the exact time someone asks you a question, resist the temptation to answer.

3. True

It's not acceptable to use one publicly after you finish eating.

4. False

The only exception is if the person who made the request insists that you take a portion for yourself prior to passing it along. Remember to pass the entire serving dish, and not just a portion.

5. ♭. When the host picks up his or her fork to begin eating

6. ♭. On the table to the left of your plate.
This can also be a signal to the waitstaff that you are done.

7. *c*. On the small plate to your left, then break off a bite-sized piece and butter it.

8. *a*. In the middle of your dinner plate, fork pointing down, knife alongside.

9. *a*. Start with the utensils farthest out from your plate and work your way in with each course.

10. *c*. Place your silverware on your dinner plate, fork, spoon, and knife resting normally.

Leaving your fork with the tines face up indicates that you're still eating—especially helpful if you step away from the table for any reason.

WEDDING ETIQUETTE

Many people spend more time in planning the wedding than they do in planning the marriage.

— ZIG ZIGLAR

1. Should you bring a gift to an engagement party?

    a. Yes, convention requires that you always bring one.

    b. There is no set rule; inquire first.

    c. Never, it is considered rude to provide gifts before the wedding.

2. As a guest at a wedding, what do you say to the new bride in the reception line?

    a. You look wonderful.

    b. Best wishes.

    c. Congratulations!

    d. I hope you have a long and excellent marriage.

3. Which of the following are among the duties of the best man?

a. Supervising the ushers

b. Carrying the bride's ring and the marriage certificate

c. Proposing the first toast to the new couple

d. Ensuring that the new couple takes off for the honeymoon without problems

e. All of the above

4. (True/False) It's expected that the groom should pay for the tuxedo rentals of the best man and groomsmen.

WHAT WILL THE GROOM PAY FOR?

The groom should be prepared to spend some money as well. Here's what he should budget and pay for:
- The bride's rings
- The marriage license
- Officiant's fee
- His formalwear
- Personal flowers: the bride's bouquet, boutonnieres for the wedding party, corsages for mothers and grandmothers
- Gifts for the groomsmen
- Wedding gift for the bride
- Gifts for parents
- Honeymoon
- Transportation to the honeymoon

5. In a typical wedding, the groom's family is expected to pay for which of the following:

   a. Flowers for ceremony and reception sites

   b. Photography

   c. Ceremony

   d. Reception

   e. Rehearsal dinner

→ WHAT EXACTLY DOES THE BEST MAN DO?

You're going to be a busy man, if you're the *best* man. There's a lot to do, and that's the whole point. If you're the best man, you're probably a close friend of the groom, and willing to help one of your best buddies during this stressful time of need. Start with supervising the ushers. Along with you, they'll be seating the guests as they arrive. In a typical Christian wedding, the groom's family and friends will be seated on the right side (facing the altar), and the bride's family and guests will be on the left. Just so you're thoroughly confused, it's all reversed at a Jewish wedding. To determine where to seat guests, simply inquire as to whether they are friends or relatives of the bride or groom when they arrive. As an usher, present your right arm to the lady while escorting her to her seat. If the woman already has a male escort, you still present your arm—and her escort follows a few steps behind. This tradition is not etched in stone though. You can simply say to the couple, "Please follow me," and then direct them to their seats.

As far as the ring is concerned, you've probably seen TV or

movie comedies where the best man fails to present the ring when prompted—feverishly checking every pocket in hopes that the ring will turn up. Just so you don't replay this routine in reality, wrap the ring in a small cloth or tissue (so it won't fall through any hole in your pocket) and keep it in your front left pocket.

During the reception, you'll also be expected to offer the first toast to the newly married couple. This usually occurs after all the guests have been seated for the meal. Tradition holds that you stand, and then grab everyone's attention by clicking on the side of your water glass with a spoon. When you have their attention, begin your (well-rehearsed) speech. In your discourse, you'll want to include something flattering about the bride, something humorous about the groom, and perhaps a memory about the couple together, e.g., the circumstances when they met, or something you observed about how in love they are. Finally, finish your toast with a sincere wish that their lives will be full of happiness and prosperity.

As if all of this weren't enough, you'll also be expected to make sure that the married couple safely departs for their destination—be it the honeymoon, or simply back to their home. Often, this involves a (pre-arranged) limousine or car with a driver. When they finally depart, take a moment to actually enjoy the wedding!

THE ANSWER KEY

1. *b.* There is no set rule; inquire first.

Unlike in a wedding—where giving a gift is usually considered appropriate—there is no set rule for an engagement party. Simply ask the host/hostess ahead of time, if gift-giving is not specified in the written invitation.

2. *b.* Best wishes.

Better not say congratulations! That's what you're supposed to say to the groom—the theory being that he has "landed" an outstanding woman—a feat for which he should be "congratulated." To the bride, you are always giving her your "best wishes," for a long and prosperous union.

3. *e.* All of the above

4. False

Whether you're a groomsman or the best man, you—not the groom— will be expected to pay for the tuxedo rental. Keep in mind that even if you already own a tuxedo, it may not be the appropriate style for the wedding. Usually, the groom will have a specific tuxedo rental store in mind, and may have already picked out an exact style.

5. *e.* Rehearsal dinner

BUSINESS ETIQUETTE

Politeness and consideration for others is like investing pennies and getting dollars back.

—THOMAS SOWELL, CREATORS SYNDICATE

Perhaps the most vital area of etiquette involves the ways in which you handle yourself in business environments. Yes, you might start in the proverbial mailroom, but if you want to succeed in any company, your business manners better reflect the best practices of the *boardroom*. Making the right impression will favorably impact your ability to get ahead for years to come.

1.   (True/False) You invite one of your vendors to lunch. As you are the customer, it's appropriate for him to pick up the tab.

2.   You're about to introduce a senior executive to a junior executive. It's appropriate to introduce them in this manner:
     a. Mr. Senior Executive, this is Mr. Junior Executive.
     b. Mr. Junior Executive, this is Mr. Senior Executive.
     c. Start with the person who extends his hand first.

When introducing one or two people to a group, always introduce the "group" to the individual(s). For example, "Bill, Joe, Sarah, and Julie, I'd like you to meet Kate."

Follow these rules in *social* situations: Always introduce the man to the woman, e.g. "Jerry, please take a moment to meet my good friend Jessica." When introducing two people of greatly different ages, always introduce the younger person to the older one, e.g. "Grandpa, I'd like you to meet my best friend from school, Joey Smith."

3. (True/False) At business functions requiring name badges, the badge should always be worn on your left side.

4. Someone is about to give *you* a toast and everyone begins to stand. You should
   a. Stand with them as a sign of respect
   b. Wait to see if the toaster gestures to you to stand
   c. Remain seated

5. The most important elements of a proper handshake are
   a. Neutral expression, wait for him to extend his hand, shake twice
   b. Smile, grasp palm-to-palm, look the person in the eye, pump three times, say his name
   c. Smile, grasp gently, look the person in the eye, pump four to five times

THE ANSWER KEY

1. False

Even though you're the customer, if you did the inviting, you should expect to pay. If the vendor insists on paying, however, reluctantly give in—but state that you had expected to pay because the invitation for lunch came from you.

2. *a*. Mr. Senior Executive, this is Mr. Junior Executive.
Seniority rules here.

3. False

When you're extending your hand for a handshake (and looking to grasp the other person's), his name tag will be in the same line of sight, making it easier for you to read it without being too obvious.

4. *c*. Remain seated

Always remain seated when someone is toasting you, as it's a sign of humility and respect. To do otherwise, would seem egotistical—as you would be lauding yourself. You should not drink at the conclusion of the toast either. If you would like to respond by offering another toast, by all means stand up while you are doing it.

5. ♭. Smile, grasp palm-to-palm, look the person in the eye, pump three times, say his or her name

When shaking hands, be sure to greet the other person by name, such as, "Very nice to meet you, Mr. Norton." Not only is this respectful, but saying his name out loud will help you to remember it at a later time.

DATING AND RELATIONSHIPS

Where love is concerned, too much is not even enough.

— PIERRE DE BEAUMARCHAIS

In the old days dating was kind of simple: you were told whom to marry—whether you liked her or not! In modern times, you may have more liberties in dating, and with that brings more complications. There are now countless ways to meet a girl, e.g., online, speed-dating, at church, through close friends, in a bar, at work, or even randomly on the street. No matter which method you use for the introduction, be prepared to follow dating rules if you want to have a successful first (and subsequent) encounter.

1. In online situations, women lie most often about which three things?

    a. Weight

    b. Income

    c. Height

    d. Marital status

    e. Age

    f. Physical build

2. When accompanying a woman down a set of stairs or on an escalator, where should you stand?

   a. Behind her

   b. Alongside her

   c. In front of her

3. You called a girl to ask her on a date and left a message, but she hasn't returned your call. What should you do?

   a. Call her again, but no more than twice.

   b. Call her again and leave an "I'm sorry, but if I don't hear from you, this is the last time I'm calling" message.

   c. Try to get a mutual friend or acquaintance to ask her why she didn't return the call.

   d. Don't call again.

→ HOW CAN YOU TELL IF SHE'S INTO YOU?

The famous researcher and professor of psychology, Albert Mehrabian, once postulated that there are three elements in play with face-to-face communication, each bearing a certain weight: words (7%), tone of voice (38%), and body language (55%). Given this, a woman may be saying one thing to you, while meaning something completely different. When a woman is trying to get a man's attention, she may reveal this via body language in one or more clues. If she's nervous about making a good impression, she may try to get rid of some of the nervous energy by fidgeting a bit, toying with a necklace, a ring, her hair, or even chewing on her lips. She may also laugh and smile more—regardless of whether you're even funny!

If she's even past the point of interest—and perhaps even on to lust—look for sassy poses (with her chest or hips out), heavier breathing, and any efforts to touch you. Eye contact will increase and her pupils will dilate.

If she's *not* into you, however, look for signs of disinterest like crossed arms, less eye contact, leaning away from you, and predictably—few or no smiles.

4. (True/False) It's customary to allow the woman to enter a cab or limousine first.

5. (True/False) You enter a room first, and then your date.

6. When walking together with a woman on the sidewalk, where should you be?
   a. On the side farther from the street
   b. On the side closer to the street
   c. Four steps behind her

7. Should you open doors and pull out chairs for women on dates?
   a. Yes, without asking
   b. Only if she shows approval
   c. Always, regardless of the situation

8. Traditionally, who should pay on the first date?

a. You

b. Your date

c. Split the tab

d. The person who asked for the date

9. What is the minimum tip you should leave at a restaurant (assuming the service was acceptable)?

a. 10%

b. 15%

c. 20%

d. 25%

10. A survey by Yahoo Personals and TheKnot.com asked women what was *most* important to them when searching for a significant other. The top answer was

a. Politics

b. Income

c. Religion

d. Work/life habits

e. Family orientation/closeness

f. Social life

g. Age

h. Ethnicity

i. Profession

11. The same survey compared online daters with offline daters and found that online daters led offline daters in reaching which of the following relationship milestones faster?

a. Initial dating

b. Feeling chemistry

c. Getting exclusive faster

d. Engagement

e. Marriage

f. All of the above

g. None of the above

12. After an initial encounter, it takes a man _____ minutes to determine whether he wants to see a woman again.

a. 2

b. 15

c. 30

d. 60

13. After an initial encounter, it takes a woman _____ minutes to determine whether she wants to see a man again.

a. 2

b. 15

c. 30

d. 60

WHAT IS YOUR BEST SOURCE FOR POTENTIAL DATES?

While Internet sites, professional dating services, and civic organizations can all be great ways to meet people, nothing beats a personal recommendation, especially when it comes to potential relationships. Your friends and colleagues know you best, and are therefore in a position to "build you up" to a potential date. Single women (and men) are more apt to believe the opinion of a friend, rather than what is portrayed about a person on an impersonal Internet site or a dating service.

14. (True/False) You should always ask permission before attempting the first kiss.

15. In modern dating, how long should you wait before calling a girl back after getting her number?
   a. 2 hours
   b. 1 day
   c. 3 days
   d. 4 days

16. You've decided to break off your engagement. What happens to the ring?
   a. You should get it back.
   b. She should keep it.

THE ANSWER KEY

1. a, e, f. Weight; Age; Physical build

   Men also tend to lie about their ages when portraying themselves online, but their next two most common untruths are usually their income and height.

2. c. In front of her

   Here's an exception to the "ladies first" rule. You want to stand in front of your woman just in case she slips or loses her footing. If she stumbles, you'll be right there to catch her.

3. d. Don't call again.

   You're done. For whatever reason, the girl (at least at present) is not interested in returning your call. The worst thing you can do at this point is to keep calling her. This would only leave her with the impression that you're desperate for a relationship.

4. False

   Getting in before her allows you to check things out and determine if the transportation is safe for her as well.

5. False

   Your date enters a room first, and you follow her.

6. *b.* On the side closer to the street

By walking between her and the street, you are theoretically in a position to push her away from the path of an out-of-control car or other threat.

7. *c.* Always, regardless of the situation

8. *d.* The person who asked for the date

Even so, a true gentleman may offer to pay for half.

9. *b.* 15%

If the service was less than satisfactory, you may consider leaving only 10%, politely informing the management, or just refrain from coming back.

10. *e.* Family orientation/closeness

44% of women surveyed responded that family closeness was most important when considering a significant other. Religion came in second with 17% and income was ranked least important, with just 1% of votes.

11. *f.* All of the above

12. *b.* 15

13. *d.* 60

14. False

Never ask permission to kiss a girl on your first date (or on whatever occasion you choose to first kiss her). If you do, you may appear to lack confidence, and even if she likes you, she may be too uncomfortable at that point to even say "yes." Just trust your instincts, and sense how your date is going. If she keeps making references to being dead-tired and wanting to go home—that's not a good sign to pucker up! However, if you believe that you're both getting along well, simply find the most appropriate moment, and then lean in for a kiss.

15. *c.* 3 days

You don't want to look desperate! And hopefully she'll spend that time wondering if you're going to call at all, and then be even more excited to hear from you.

16. *a.* You should get it back.

WAKES AND FUNERALS

Even the best of friends cannot attend each other's funeral.

— KEHLOG ALBRAN

Attending wakes and funerals is probably one of the most dreaded activities you'll have to face. Hopefully, you won't have to go to many, but attending funerals of people who were close to you (or perhaps close to your friends/relatives) is an essential part of manhood. It's quite normal to feel scared, confused, and a bit unsure of yourself, and virtually everyone at a funeral is experiencing this to some extent. Understanding proper funeral etiquette is not only a sign of respect, but knowing the rituals will help you to minimize the emotional turmoil.

1. (True/False) During a condolence visit to a family's home, it's best not to share any memories of the deceased as you don't want to stir emotions.

2. (True/False) It's no longer mandatory to wear only black clothing at a funeral.

3. The job of a pallbearer is to

 a. Seat people at the funeral as they arrive

 b. Stay by the relatives as an aide

 c. Help carry (or more often "wheel") the casket

4. (True/False) According to tradition, the wake usually takes place after the funeral service.

THE ANSWER KEY

1. False

   By sharing stories, you're both honoring the deceased's memory and giving others a sense of what that person meant to you.

2. True

   While you don't need to dress all in black, you should wear darker clothing and perhaps a conservative tie. Funerals are all about the deceased, and any clothing combination that focuses on you defeats the point.

3. *c.* Help carry (or more often "wheel") the casket

4. False

   In earlier times, friends and relatives actually stayed "awake" with the body of the deceased until it was delivered to the cemetery. Their task was to search for any signs of life before the person was laid to rest. Today, the purpose of a wake is for mourners to gather, share memories, and to say "goodbye" to the loved one. Although grief and sadness is to be expected, the wake may also take the form of a party to help celebrate the departed's life.

CAREER AND EMPLOYMENT

DID YOU INHERIT a huge fortune or win the Powerball lottery? If not, you'll need to know how to locate—and then retain—a good job. Your overall happiness may depend on how well your job fits *you*. No matter how much money a job pays, full-time misery at any occupation can be excruciating. Even after you find the right job, the size of your salary (and your benefits) will depend on how well you negotiate your compensation package. Test your knowledge on the best ways to find your dream job and maximize your earnings.

YOUR RÉSUMÉ

What is the recipe for successful achievement? To my mind there are just four essential ingredients: Choose a career you love, give it the best there is in you, seize your opportunities, and be a member of the team.

— BENJAMIN F. FAIRLESS

1. The primary purpose of a résumé is to
   a. Get you a job
   b. Get you an interview
   c. List your accomplishments for an employer's consideration

2. (True/False) In the Professional Objectives section of your résumé, it's okay to list several different career objectives.

3. (True/False) Your GPA is a 2.8 (out of 4). You should not reveal this on your résumé.

4. (True/False) As long as you look presentable, it's important to include a photograph either on, or with, your résumé.

5. When describing your past job experiences, it's best to use what type of words, and why?

a. Nouns, as you should stick solely to the facts

b. Action verbs, as they imply accomplishment

c. Adjectives, as they describe how you went about your job

6. (True/False) You don't need to list all of your work experiences on a résumé.

7. The most important feature of an electronic résumé is

a. The use of keywords

b. Inclusion of references

c. Absence of formal formatting

d. Exclusion of a picture

8. (True/False) It's okay to send the same résumé to different companies.

9. (True/False) It's acceptable to simply print "References are available upon request" rather than listing them on your résumé.

THE ANSWER KEY

1. *b.* Get you an interview

   Virtually all employers want to screen applicants personally before making a hiring decision. The primary purpose of your résumé is to spark enough interest so they'll want to see you in person.

2. False

   If you're considering more than one career, compose a different résumé (and professional objective) for each one.

3. True

   The last thing you want to do is highlight mediocrity in your résumé!

4. False

   Unless a picture is specifically requested, don't include one.

5. *b.* Action verbs

   Ask yourself, "What problem(s) did I solve at my previous job?" Then, list these problem-solving accomplishments on your résumé— beginning with action verbs.

   - **Doubled** *sales from previous year*
   - **Created** *cost-cutting program that saved the company $1,000,000*
   - **Improved** *product placements in stores by 50%*

- **Developed** *computer program for better customer relations*
- **Consolidated** *two departments into one to save costs*

6. True

This is especially true if past jobs are not pertinent to your current job search.

7. *a*. The use of keywords

Keywords are words or phrases that employers search for to screen the right candidates for a job. They describe your skills, experience, education level, and any special abilities. Examples of keywords are sales, MBA, e-commerce, business development, schedule management, financial reports, Excel, investor relations, Word, teambuilding, etc. Using the right keywords in your résumé may help you survive the first screening process, and perhaps get you an interview. Conversely, if you don't have the right keywords, your résumé is likely to get tossed in the trash—by a computer.

8. True

But be sure to customize each cover letter!

9. True

It's acceptable to simply print "References are available upon request."

JOB HUNTING

1. Which is the most effective way of getting a job?

   a. Sending résumés to companies using school recruiting offices

   b. Answering newspaper ads, and using job agencies

   c. Visiting companies and talking with supervisors and employees

2. How many companies does the average person typically visit before landing a job?

   a. 1–3

   b. 4–6

   c. 7–9

   d. 10–70

3. How long can you expect to search before you get a job?

   a. 1–3 days

   b. 4–10 days

   c. 2–4 weeks

   d. 2–6 months

4. Which question(s) are illegal for the company to ask you in an interview?

   a. Do you have any disabilities?

   b. What is your greatest strength?

   c. What is your five-year goal?

   d. What race are you?

5. When an interviewer asks, "What are your weaknesses?" you should

   a. Spin a negative into a positive, e.g., "I work constantly, even at home."

   b. Avoid answering it, and just mention a few of your strengths

   c. Be honest and try not to avoid answering the question

6. The interviewer states that he's narrowed his decision on giving this job to you, or one other candidate. What's the best way to handle this?

   a. Ask details about the other person so you can compare.

   b. Summarize your strong points.

   c. Ask to be interviewed along with him or her in the same room.

7. The interviewer asks, "Where do you see yourself in five years?" You should

   a. Impress him with your determination by saying that you'd like to own a company like his *b.* Reveal your intentions by stating you'd like your boss's job

c. Talk in general terms about excelling at your job so you'll be considered for new opportunities

d. Reveal your long-term goal about working in a different industry

THE ANSWER KEY

1. *c.* Visiting companies and talking with supervisors and employees

   A great résumé is obviously an important tool, but face-to-face meetings are far more effective in gaining career opportunities. As much as 80% of all job openings are filled through (direct and indirect) referrals, not through job postings.

2. *d.* 10–70

3. *d.* 2–6 months

4. *a, d.* Do you have any disabilities?; What race are you?

   It is permissible though to inquire about your physical ability to perform a particular job function, e.g., stacking heavy boxes.

5. *c.* Be honest and try not to avoid answering the question

   If you're dodging a question, you may come across as being shifty or disingenuous. Be honest about your challenges, yet use some examples about how you've managed to work on them.

6. *b.* Summarize your strong points

   Asking questions about the other candidate will only make you look weak and insecure.

7. *c.* Talk in general terms about excelling at your job so you'll be considered for new opportunities

It's okay to have aspirations such as wanting a job promotion, but this is no place to be cocky by exclaiming that you'd like to own their business!

NEGOTIATING A SALARY

I am indeed rich, since my income is superior to my expenses, and my expense is equal to my wishes.

— EDWARD GIBBON

1. When interviewing for a job, your prospective employer states that the salary range is between $50,000 and $60,000. You should
   a. Say nothing
   b. Try to negotiate the higher figure after you've been offered the job
   c. Ask, "Is $60,000 the best you can offer?"

2. In a job interview, your prospective employer asks you what your current (or last) salary is. You should
   a. State the figure honestly, as he will probably verify it
   b. Say something like, "My salary is within the industry range for my qualifications"
   c. Try to gingerly change the subject

3. You've been working for the same company for a while, but another company has offered you a job with a higher salary. You gave your departure notice but your current company has counter-offered with even more money to convince you to stay. You should

a. Stay with your current company with the higher salary

b. Take the job offer and leave

c. Tell the new company to match what your current company is now offering

4. You're at an impasse, and the employer won't raise the salary offer to an amount acceptable to you. You should

a. End the negotiation, and look for employment elsewhere

b. Accept the offer, and hope to increase your salary at a later date

c. Ask for non-salary benefits

THE ANSWER KEY

1. *c.* Ask, "Is $60,000 the best you can offer?"

The worst case result is that he says, "Yes." At this point, you've taken the lower amount completely out of play. It's even possible that he'll respond with something like, "Well, we might *be able to do a little better," or even offer other benefits instead.*

2. *b.* Say something like, "My salary is within the industry range for my qualifications"

Don't get suckered into stating your salary; it's never to your advantage!

3. *b.* Take the job offer and leave

Corporate recruiter Hal Reiter says, "I have learned that accepting a counter-offer is usually career suicide. Watching your boss scramble to keep you may be a heady experience, but in exchange for that sweet moment, you'll have squandered your honor, a sacrifice that will haunt you for many years."

4. *c.* Ask for non-salary benefits

Non-salary benefits bonuses can include use of a company car, an expense account, stock bonuses, etc.

HOME RENTING AND BUYING

SHOULD YOU RENT? Should you buy? What are the advantages of each? Can you afford to buy? When you start out on your own, chances are you'll probably end up renting an apartment or small home. You'll have to be careful though, as renting comes with many restrictions, and your lifestyle may suffer from the limitations imposed by your landlord. As you become more financially capable, owning may be the best option, but you have to know what you're doing to truly make a home an investment.

RENTING

I installed a skylight in my apartment...the people who live above me are furious!

— STEVEN WRIGHT, COMEDIAN

1. (True/False) When renting a home, everything you need to know about the rules and regulations is contained in your lease.

2. (True/False) You decide to get a roommate. It's okay to not inform the landlord, as long as you continue to pay your rent on time.

3. (True/False) Your dishwasher breaks. It's always the landlord's responsibility to pay for the repair.

4. (True/False) You decided to get a cat, but pets weren't mentioned in your lease. It's okay to purchase your pet, as long as you notify the landlord afterward.

5. (True/False) Your landlord believes that you've violated one or more conditions in your lease. He can change the locks on your apartment to keep you from entering.

6. You should be able to break your lease and move under which of the following circumstances?
   a. Your apartment is seriously damaged by no fault of your own.
   b. Your landlord refuses to make necessary repairs, despite your repeated requests.
   c. Your job transfers you to another city.
   d. You've been called to active military duty.
   e. Your landlord constantly invades your privacy, preventing you from quietly enjoying your apartment.

7. Which of the following criteria can the landlord legally take into consideration when deciding whether to lease to you?

a. Your race

b. Your income

c. A mental or physical disability

d. Your religion

e. Bad references from a previous landlord

f. Your national origin

g. Your sex

THE ANSWER KEY

1. False

In addition to the rules and restrictions in your lease, you may also be subject to the policies and regulations of a homeowner's association. The association might have restrictions on whether you can affix a basketball backboard to your house, park a boat in your driveway, etc. Your lease should mention the existence of a homeowner's association agreement, but it's ultimately your responsibility to find out and follow the rules that have been set up in your community.

2. False

Read your lease carefully!

3. False

Appliance repairs are often the responsibility of the landlord, but all leases are different, so read yours carefully.

4. False

Remember—check your lease!

5. False

Your landlord simply cannot lock you out of your apartment. He must first petition a court for a hearing, where you'll be given an opportunity to respond to his complaint.

6. *a, b, d, e.*

Having to move to another city because of a new job or transfer is not a valid reason for breaking your lease. You may have to pay a penalty and/or lose your deposit.

7. *b, e.* Your income; Bad references from a previous landlord. *Some states also prohibit discrimination based on age, marital status, and sexual orientation.*

OWNING A HOME

Home is the place where, when you have to go there, they have to take you in.

— ROBERT FROST

1. (True/False) Buying a home makes sense, even if you only plan to own the home for a year or so.

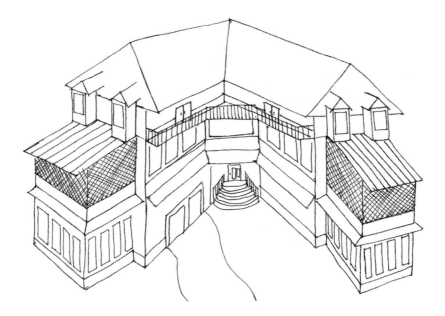

2. (True/False) Banks and mortgage companies typically offer two "term" options for your home loan: 15 or 30 years. Generally, interest rates are higher for a 15-year mortgage versus a 30-year mortgage.

3. (True/False) In a variable mortgage (versus fixed), the monthly payment may change over the term of the mortgage.

→ THE BENEFITS OF RENTING AND BUYING

Renting

When you rent, your landlord is usually responsible for fixing broken items in your apartment, such as appliances like the dishwasher and refrigerator. However, check your lease before you sign it, as you may still be responsible for some repairs, especially if they're a result of negligence. A major advantage of leasing is that you're free to move at the end of your lease—without any further obligation. Any increase in the value of your rented home or apartment, however, goes directly into your landlord's pocket.

Buying

Although there are no guarantees, your home will likely increase in value over time. Even after adjusting for inflation, the median home value in the United States has quadrupled over the last sixty years. For many people, their home ultimately becomes their largest single investment. There are times, however, when your home may actually decrease in value—as evidenced by the housing "bubble" prices over the last few years.

In most cases, you should have the ability to change the outside décor of your home, e.g., paint colors, awnings, roof tile selection, etc. You should also have control over your choice of landscaping. Be aware, however, that many communities have restrictions and/or approval processes for making changes. You realtor should inform you of these before you make a purchase decision.

Another advantage of owning your home is having a tax benefit—as you're able to deduct the home loan interest directly from your income. For example, if you earn $40,000 and the interest on your homeowner's loan is $3,000, your taxable income drops to $37,000. Less income means you'll be paying less tax.

Forget about moving quickly. Selling your home can be a lengthy process, sometimes taking up to a year or more before you secure a buyer and close the transaction.

4. You're choosing between two different lenders, and both are offering you the same interest rate on your loan. The first lender, however, is charging you 2 points on your loan and the other is not. What does this mean?

   a. The lender is making the following points: 1) don't miss your monthly payment, and 2) if you do, I'll take your house back.

   b. The lender is charging you a fee equal to 2% of the value of the home as part of the loan costs.

   c. Your credit score was 2 points lower than ideal.

5. When deciding how much you can afford to spend on a home, a general rule of thumb is

a. 10 times your annual salary

b. 5 times your annual salary

c. 2 times your annual salary

d. Half your annual salary

THE ANSWER KEY

1. False

You may actually lose a great deal of money during your first year of ownership (versus renting). The longer you plan to own your home, the more likely it will make financial sense to buy it. Check out the "buy vs. rent calculator" at www.ginniemae.gov.

2. False

Your interest rate will be lower with a 15-year mortgage, but monthly loan payments will be substantially higher, as you're paying off the obligation in half the time.

3. True

Variable mortgage means exactly that: your interest rate will likely vary over the length of your loan. If rates go down, you certainly benefit by having a lower loan payment. Conversely, if rates go up, your loan payment may escalate dramatically!

4. ♭. The lender is charging you a fee equal to 2% of the value of the home as part of the loan costs.

Mortgage points are fees that you pay as part of your loan package. One point is equal to one percentage of your loan. Often, the mortgage company will entice you into a lower interest rate by charging you these points. Generally, the longer you intend to hold your home, the more it makes sense to consider paying the points.

5. *c.* 2 times your annual salary

FINANCE AND NEGOTIATION

||||||||||||||||||||||||||||||||||||||||||||||||||||||||||||||||||||||||||||||||||||||||||||||||||||||||||||||||

HOW GOOD IS your credit and how can you improve it? Why does it matter? Banks and lending institutions not only approve loans based on your credit score, but the interest you pay will likely be directly affected as well. Simply put, a bad credit score will cost you money and may prevent you from purchasing a home or car.

CREDIT SCORE

Remember that credit is money.

— BENJAMIN FRANKLIN

Why do you need good credit? If you don't have all of the money required (or don't want to spend it) to make a large purchase such as a home or a car, you'll need to apply for credit. Even if you don't plan on making a large purchase, your credit score may be considered by potential employers and landlords as part of their review process.

1. Which of the following credit scores is the best?
   a. 379
   b. 490
   c. 625
   d. 740

2. (True/False) The higher your salary and net worth, the better your credit score.

3. Which of the following variables are not considered in constructing your credit score?
   a. Number and severity of late payments
   b. Type, number, and age of accounts

c. Your marital status

d. Total debt

e. Where you live

4. (True/False) You actually have three credit scores, not just one.

5. One of the ways to maintain a good credit score is to keep your credit card account balances below ____ of your available credit limits.

a. 10%

b. 35%

c. 70%

d. 0%—you should always pay the monthly balance in full

6. (True/False) Be careful whom you marry, as your credit scores are merged after the "I dos."

7. (True/False) Your credit score won't be negatively affected by how many credit inquiries you have (by applying for a new credit card, loan, etc.) as long as you pay off your debts in a timely manner.

8. (True/False) If you pay your credit card bill on time and in full, most credit card companies will not charge you any interest.

THE ANSWER KEY

1. *d*. 740

   The higher your credit score, the better—all the way up to 850. A good credit score is usually above 700.

2. False

   Many factors are included in calculating your credit score, like the amount of debt you have, how current you are on your debt payments, etc., but your income and net worth are not factors.

3. *c, e*. Your marital status; Where you live

4. True

   There are three major credit bureaus (Equifax, TransUnion, and Experian), and each one calculates your credit score independently. It's probably a good idea to check your score at all three bureaus, as it may vary by up to 50 points among them.

5. *b*. 35%

   If you have a limit on your credit card of $1,000, try to keep your balance below $350. When you go above this figure, expect your credit score to be negatively impacted.

6. False

Your credit scores will remain independent.

7. False

Large numbers of credit inquiries over a short period of time presents a signal to the credit industry that you may be desperate—and desperate people generally are not good credit risks.

8. True

They won't charge interest if you pay on time, every month, in full. Keep in mind, though, that most credit card companies will not *give you a grace period if you get a cash advance off your card.*

GENERAL NEGOTIATING

Let us never negotiate out of fear. But let us never fear to negotiate.

—JOHN F. KENNEDY, 35TH PRESIDENT OF THE UNITED STATES

Why negotiate? Well, the truth is—you don't have to. If you pay for what others are asking, you won't have to engage in any "back and forth" haggling. You'll also be out a lot more money and spending a great deal more over the long run than you have to.

How good are you at getting the best deal on a purchase? With the right skills, you might be able to save a few dollars off your weekly grocery bill, or perhaps thousands of dollars when buying a car or home. You may even improve your income when negotiating a salary—but to get your best deal, you need to first know the elements of a good negotiation.

1. The price of an item you want to buy is not displayed. To negotiate the best deal, you should
   a. Not ask a specific price; just offer a price you're willing to pay
   b. Ask him exactly what he wants
   c. Be vague, and talk about the price of similar items sold elsewhere

2. Each time you make a concession in a negotiation, you should

   a. Act irritated, and threaten to stop negotiating

   b. Ask for something in return

   c. Try to wrap up the negotiation at that time

3. The outcome of an ideal negotiation is

   a. You lose, they win

   b. You win, they lose

   c. You win, they win

4. What two elements are most important when negotiating any purchase?

   a. Time and information

   b. Price and color

   c. Seller's attitude and buyer's emotion

→ TIPS FOR NEGOTIATIONS

The more information you have about the party you're negotiating with, the better your chances are for a constructive negotiation. Some examples of critically important information: How desperate is the seller to make a deal? What did he or she originally pay for the item you're trying to buy? What's the lowest price at which he sold one of these to another buyer? How many does he have? Is there time pressure on the seller to make a deal?

Let's say you're looking for a home. First, find out how long the home's been listed on the market. If the seller just put the home up for sale, you're much less likely to get a great deal, as his hopes are probably high for getting his asking price. Instead, look for homes that have been for sale for six months or more. These sellers should be more desperate to sell, and may be willing to take much less than the original asking price. Find out if the seller is in a hurry to move. If he has accepted a job in another city, he's more likely to bend on price than a seller who's in no rush to leave.

Time can also be a critical factor in another way. When negotiating a purchase, try to tie up a great deal of the seller's time. The more time he invests with you, the more pressure he'll feel to conclude a deal. If you're looking at used cars, for example, try to engage the salesperson for many hours in the process. Look at a bunch of cars, and test drive as many as you can. Ask a million questions about each car: "What's the gas mileage again? How many owners has this car had? Can I see the engine compartment? How does this car do in snow?" If you spend many hours with a salesperson, he'll be dying to sell you *something*, and you can be sure he'll work extra hard to get a deal done with you.

If you want a successful negotiation, be aware that there will likely be numerous situations that arise to prevent you from keeping your eye on the ball—namely, completing the negotiation. Don't become distracted by the other person's personality, his quirks, his emotions, or his negotiating technique (or lack of it). Always ask yourself, "What's my goal?" and continue to redirect your focus back to the goal until the deal is done.

5. When the seller first states the price of something you want, you should

a. Say something like, "That's pretty reasonable," so you maintain a positive negotiation

b. Flinch, and appear amazed that the price is so high (no matter how inexpensive you might think it is)

c. Say, "You've got a deal," and complete the purchase

6. Which of the following is not considered a negative in a negotiation?

a. Trying to win at all costs

b. Failure to understand the other person

c. Blaming the other party when things aren't going well

d. Maintaining unwavering focus on the desired outcome

7. (True/False) When negotiating for anything, it always helps to get emotionally involved.

8. The most effective negotiating style is to

a. Act humble

b. Impress the seller with your knowledge and negotiating skills

c. Act overly enthusiastic

d. Be combative

e. Act suspicious

THE ANSWER KEY

1. *b*. Ask him exactly what he wants

By not asking for the price, you may end up paying more. If you start by offering what you're willing to pay (even if you think it's ridiculously low), you risk the fact that he might have quoted you an even lower price.

2. *b*. Ask for something in return

3. *c*. You win, they win

You'll leave with a positive impression from the other party, which will not only enhance your reputation, but may also benefit you in future negotiations.

4. *a*. Time and information

5. *b*. Flinch, and appear amazed that the price is so high (no matter how inexpensive you might think it is)

Always appear amazed that the price could possibly be that high, even if you feel he's practically giving it away! The seller's natural instinct is to not insult your judgment about pricing. Therefore, he'll usually come back with a statement like, "Well, we might be able to do better—let me check with the manager."

6. *d.* Maintaining unwavering focus on the desired outcome

7. False

You want to stay emotionally neutral when negotiating a purchase. The moment you say to yourself, "I have to have this," you've lost. Your ability to negotiate a great deal from that moment on is compromised, as you've lost the walk away option.

8. *a.* Act humble

If you try to impress someone with your negotiating skills, you may energize the other party to stand firm—for he'll want to know he wasn't taken advantage of by a real "pro."

NEGOTIATING A CAR PURCHASE

Everything in life is somewhere else, and you get there in a car.

— E. B. WHITE

Next to your home, your second-largest expenditure in your life will probably be the amount you spend on automobiles. Knowing how to negotiate a car purchase may save you thousands of dollars on each purchase, and perhaps tens of thousands of dollars over the long term. Beware, as the automobile industry is well known for shady practices and misrepresentations. You need to be a savvy and informed negotiator to get your best deal.

1. (True/False) The dealer invoice (a.k.a. factory invoice) is the amount the car dealer paid the manufacturer for your vehicle.

2. One of the best days to negotiate a car purchase at a dealer is the
   a. 1st day of a month
   b. 15th day of a month
   c. Last day of a month
   d. Doesn't matter

3. (True/False) If you trade in your car while purchasing another one, in most states you only pay sales tax on the difference between the cost of the new car and the value of your trade-in.

4. (True/False) You're likely to negotiate a better price from a dealer when you offer all cash versus telling him you intend to finance the car.

5. A new car will likely go down in value as much as ____% the minute you drive it off the lot.
   a. 2
   b. 4
   c. 7
   d. 20

6. (True/False) You typically pay a higher monthly payment when you lease a car versus buying it outright.

7. Both leasing and buying a car (with a loan) share this expense in common:
   a. Principal charge
   b. Finance charge
   c. Depreciation charge

8. When buying a car, you're most likely to negotiate which of the following:

a. Sales tax

b. Dealer preparation fees

c. Destination charges

d. Registration fees

e. All of the above

THE ANSWER KEY

1. False

The dealer (or factory) invoice is theoretically the price that the dealer pays the manufacturer for the car, prior to selling it to you. Many times, dealers will reveal the factory invoice price to the buyers, implying that they are "not making much profit" on the car they're trying to sell you. The dealer's actual cost, however, will be less than the factory invoice figure, due to expected holdbacks, factory rebates, and bonuses from the manufacturer.

2. The last day of the month

Car dealers generally gauge how well their sales are doing based on monthly sales cycles.

3. True

You only pay on the differential between the amount you sold for and the amount you spent.

4. False

Nearly all new car dealers have Finance and Insurance departments (F&I) that offer to help you secure financing (and perhaps insurance) for your vehicle. When he writes your loan, the dealer receives a hefty commission from the finance company—adding profits to the car transaction.

5. *d.* 20

That "new car smell" can be very expensive! A vehicle's value immediately drops from the retail price to the wholesale price when it leaves the lot.

6. False

When you lease, payments are lower, as you're only paying for the part of the vehicle you "use" (usually the first 3 years). When you buy a car, you're paying for (or financing) the entire *purchase of the vehicle.*

7. *b.* Finance charge

8. *b.* Dealer preparation fees

These charges are supposed to represent the labor and supplies (washing and vacuuming the car, removing plastic seat covers, adding oil and transmission fluid) associated with preparing the vehicle to make it presentable for sale. Since all of these items are both inexpensive and only take a few hours to complete, a dealer should be open to removing, or at least reducing part of this expense.

INVESTING

How many millionaires do you know who have become
wealthy by investing in savings accounts? I rest
my case.

— ROBERT G. ALLEN

Why invest? Why not just save? Saving usually involves putting your money in relatively riskless places like a bank savings account, but your expected returns are small—so small that they may not even keep up with inflation. Investing, on the other hand, usually involves some risk of losing part or all of your investment, but with expected higher returns. John Hancock Mutual Funds, Inc., states, "…it's hard to imagine that you can achieve your long-term goals without investing. History shows that investing in the stock and bond markets provides greater returns than most investors can earn through guaranteed savings." Given this, you should probably become familiar with how to invest in a careful way that increases your wealth, while at the same time minimizing risk.

Your ultimate financial goal for retirement (*whatever* age that occurs) should be to reach "critical mass"—a financial benchmark whereby you can live off your investments, rather than working. Simply put, it's when the interest and returns on your money, stocks, ls, etc., provide enough income so you don't have to rely on a salary. To get there, however, you'll need to become a savvy investor.

1. Corporate stocks are
   a. Debt that a company owes to someone
   b. Inventory a company keeps on hand
   c. Ownership shares of a company

2. Corporate dividends are:
   a. Funds distributed by a company to its shareholders
   b. Special bonds that companies sell to shareholders
   c. Repayment of debts to the company's creditors

3. A bond is
   a. A share of ownership in a company
   b. A pledge by the company to shareholders
   c. A debt obligation of a company

4. (True/False) As a rule, bonds are riskier investments than stocks.

5. A good rule of thumb for the percentage of stocks you own in your overall investment portfolio is
   a. Your age plus 20
   b. 100 minus your age
   c. Your age times 2

6. Rank the following investments from the highest expected return to the lowest.

   a. Bonds, stocks, money market

   b. Money market, stocks, bonds

   c. Stocks, bonds, money market

7. (True/False) You can lose your entire investment in a stock purchase.

8. The average investment return for stocks over the last 100 years is approximately

   a. –15%

   b. –11%

   c. 2.7%

   d. 9.3%

9. A CD (certificate of deposit) is

   a. A statement the bank gives you after making a checking deposit

   b. A specialized deposit you make at a bank or other financial institution

   c. A type of stock that pays you exceptional dividends

10. A money market fund is

   a. A high-yielding account at a bank

   b. A type of mutual fund that invests in low-risk securities *c.* Funds retained at your supermarket for groceries

  d. A fund that owns various stocks

11. A mutual fund is

  a. A joint bank account between two people

  b. A collection of various stocks and/or bonds and other assets

  c. An assortment of bank accounts that pay interest

12. (True/False) Over time, due to fund expenses, nearly 80% of mutual funds underperform the returns of the stock market.

THE ANSWER KEY

1. *c*. Ownership shares of a company

   Shares of stock represent a fraction of ownership in a business. When you buy a share of stock, you are buying a part of that company (however small that may be). For example, let's say a company is worth $1,000, and they issued 100 shares of stock. Each share is worth 1% of the company's value, or $10.

2. *a*. Funds distributed by a company to its shareholders

   When companies make money, they often distribute these profits in the form of dividends to their shareholders.

3. *c*. A debt obligation of a company

   Bonds are issued by a company (or a government entity) where investors loan it money. In return, they promise to pay the money back at a specified time, while paying investors interest (called the coupon rate) until the bond matures (the payback date).

4. False

   Generally, bonds are less risky than stocks, but they're not without risk. A company that's in trouble may not be able to pay the bond in full, or on time. The riskier the bond, generally the higher the interest rate paid.

5. *b*. 100 minus your age

6. *c.* Stocks, bonds, money market

Stocks are generally the highest risk, followed by bonds and then money market funds.

7. True

You can lose your entire investment in a stock purchase.

8. *d.* 9.3%

Stocks should be viewed as a long-term investment, and over time the stocks you own can be a profitable part of your investment strategy.

9. *b.* A specialized deposit you make at a bank or other financial institution

10. *b.* A type of mutual fund that invests in low-risk securities

Low-risk securities include short-term bonds, government securities, etc.

11. *b.* A collection of various stocks and/or bonds and other assets.

Purchasing shares in mutual funds is considered less risky than owning individual stocks or bonds, etc., as you are spreading your risk over a group of diverse assets, rather than one individual investment.

12. True

Nearly 80% of mutual funds underperform the stock market averages, due to the costs of running these funds.

TRANSPORTATION

||||||||||||||||||||||||||||||||||||||||||||||||||||||||||||||||||||||||||||||||||

UNLESS YOU PLAN on spending the rest of your life at home, you'll need to know the basics of getting from one place to another. Most of the time, you'll likely be traveling in something that has wheels, wings, or a hull. Depending on the mode of transportation, you'll need to know specific rules in order to get to your final destination. When traveling by boat, for example, why should you care which side is the starboard and which is the port? Well, if you're on a sinking cruise ship, it may help when the captain announces that the only remaining lifeboat is on the starboard side. And what if you missed your flight because you were delayed by security for carrying an item that you didn't realize was prohibited? Just as important, you should be able to perform basic maintenance on your car, or you may find yourself stranded on the side of the road somewhere.

PLANES

Why don't they make the whole plane out of that black box stuff?

— STEVEN WRIGHT, COMEDIAN

1. In order to pass through airport security, all liquids, gels, and aerosols must be in ___ ounce or smaller containers.
   a. 1.5
   b. 3.4
   c. 16.2
   d. 24.5

2. All liquids, gels, and aerosols must be placed in a single, ____-size, zip-top, clear plastic bag.
   a. 10 oz.
   b. 16 oz.
   c. 1 qt.
   d. 1 gal.

3. (True/False) Reasonable quantities greater than 3 ounces of prescription and/or over-the-counter medications are allowed through the security checkpoint.

4. (True/False) For domestic travel, you may bring firearms and ammunition in your checked baggage.

5. Which of the following is *not* an acceptable identification for airport clearance?

a. State license

b. Passport

c. Major credit card with photo

d. State identification card

6. Which of the following items are *not* allowed through airport security?

a. Bic-style cigarette lighter

b. Strike-anywhere matches

c. 7-inch-long screwdriver

d. Hammer

e. Nail clippers

7. (True/False) It's permissible to carry a book of safety matches with you through airport security, but it's *not* permitted to pack them in your checked luggage.

8. Which of the following items are allowed through airport security as carry-ons on a commercial aircraft?

a. Baseball bats

b. Bows and arrows

c. Cricket bats

d. Golf clubs

e. Hockey sticks

f. Lacrosse sticks

g. Pool cues

h. Ski poles

i. Spear guns

j. None of the above

9. For domestic travel, the typical maximum weight of a checked-in bag (without a financial penalty levied by the airline) is ____ lbs.

a. 10

b. 25

c. 50

d. 75

THE ANSWER KEY

1. *b.* 3.4

   3.4 ounces of anything (about one-third of a can of soda) is not that much, but that's the point. The TSA doesn't want anyone to bring a large quantity of anything that could be dangerous in any way, e.g., bomb-making materials or flammable liquids.

2. *c.* 1 qt.

3. True

   If you need a larger quantity of your medication, the TSA will allow you to bring it on board. Also, if you're traveling with a small child, you may bring larger quantities of baby formula, breast milk, juices, etc.

4. True

   Don't try to take a firearm through the security checkpoint, but you can keep it in your checked luggage if you
   - *Declare it to the airline during the check-in process*
   - *Make sure the gun is unloaded*
   - *Make sure it's in a locked, hard-sided container*

5. *c.* Major credit card with photo

You may also use a military ID, Native American Tribal Photo ID, Permanent Resident Card, or Border Crossing Card.

6. b, d. Strike-anywhere matches; Hammer

Yes, screwdrivers are allowed, but only if they're 7 inches long or shorter.

7. True

It's permissible to carry a book of safety matches with you through airport security, but it's not permitted to pack them in your checked luggage.

8. j. None of the above

Although all are permitted in your checked luggage.

9. *c.* 50 lbs.

AUTOMOBILES

I've got two old Volvos, two old Subarus, and an old Ford Ranger. If you've got an old car, you've gotta have at least several old cars, 'cause one's always gonna be in the garage.

— RIP TORN, ACTOR

1. Fuel flows from the gas tank to your engine by
   a. Osmosis
   b. Reverse osmosis
   c. Electric or mechanical fuel pump
   d. Gravity

2. The function of a fuel injector is to
   a. Mix oil with fuel
   b. Mix air with fuel
   c. Apply steering fluid as needed
   d. Change the engine's operating temperature

3. How often should you rotate your tires?

    a. 1,000–2,000 miles

    b. 3,000–5,000 miles

    c. 5,000–10,000 miles

    d. 12,000–18,000 miles

4. Your car begins to make squealing, chirping, or grinding noises. What does this typically indicate?

    a. Your tires need replacing.

    b. Your engine is running out of oil.

    c. Your engine is running out of gas.

    d. Your brakes are worn.

5. The master cylinder is

    a. A holding tank for brake fluid

    b. The primary cylinder in your car's engine

    c. A cylindrical tube that holds both tires to the rear axle

6. Under normal driving conditions, how often should you change your oil?

    a. 2,000 miles

    b. 5,000 miles

    c. 7,500 miles

    d. 18,000 miles

7. Which grade of oil is least appropriate for your vehicle if you live in a cold climate?

    a. 5W-30

    b. 10W-30

    c. 20W-40

8. Improper tire inflation will cause which of the following?

    a. Improper wear on your tire

    b. Poor engine performance

    c. Deteriorated gas mileage

    d. High oil pressure

    e. Poor car handling

    f. Compromised braking

9. The three primary filters in your car are

    a. Air, oil, fuel

    b. Fuel, water, steering fluid

    c. Water, air, radiator fluid

10. What's the purpose of a car's transmission?

    a. Transmit engine data to your dashboard gauges

    b. Mitigate between engine RPM (revolutions per minute) and wheel RPM

    c. Regulate oil temperature

11. What is the function of the car's radiator?

    a. Introduce radiation into the engine

    b. Cool the fluid that circulates the engine

    c. Increase tire pressure when necessary

    d. Turn the radio on and off

12. (True/False) You need to tow your car. It's okay to tie a chain directly to your front bumper.

THE ANSWER KEY

1. *c*. Electric or mechanical fuel pump

2. *b*. Mix air with fuel

Your car is propelled forward by a series of controlled explosions in your engine's cylinders. Gasoline—without oxygen—is not flammable, let alone explosive. The purpose of a fuel injector is to mix the precise amount of gas and oxygen (air) to create the ideal explosion in your car's cylinders.

3. *c*. 5,000–10,000 miles

To accommodate for uneven wear, your tires must be periodically rotated to different wheels. Check your tire manufacturer's recommendation to be sure.

4. *d*. Your brakes are worn.

Get out your wallet, as you're probably going to need new brake pads—and perhaps even rotors.

5. *a*. A holding tank for brake fluid

6. *c*. 7,500 miles

Typically oil should be changed every 7,500 miles, but refer to your specific auto manual. Oil lubricates your engine, reducing—but not eliminating—the wear of metal-on-metal in your engine's moving parts. This friction in your engine creates micro-particles of metal that circulate throughout your engine in the oil. Over time, these metal shavings can create long-term damage to your engine. Your car's oil filter removes the bulk of these particles.

7. *c*. 20W-40

Oils are manufactured in many varieties for different engines and driving conditions. The lower the number in front of the "W," the easier the oil flows when the engine is cold. The number after the dash indicates the viscosity (thickness) of the oil at the engine's operating temperature (when hot). Oils that remain thicker at operating temperature somewhat reduce fuel efficiency, but they also protect the engine by helping to maintain a proper oil pressure. The ideal oil is one that is thin enough to operate when an engine first starts—yet thick enough to work reliably when the engine is really hot. Given this, you wouldn't want to use a 20W oil in a cold climate, as the oil is simply too thick to operate properly in a cold engine.

8. *a, c, e, f.* Improper wear on your tire; Deteriorated gas mileage; Poor car handling; Compromised braking

When your tires are overinflated, less tire surface touches the ground, compromising their ability to "hug" the road. This also causes your car to "bounce"—separating your vehicle completely from the road surface. In addition to poor handling, you lose traction, lessening your ability to stop the vehicle properly. Underinflated tires cause problems as well. First, they develop excess heat, which could lead to total tire failure. They also wear improperly, negatively affecting handling, and can cost you up to a mile per gallon in lost fuel economy.

9. a. Air, oil, fuel.
Air and fuel filters insure that your vehicle's engine burns only a clean mixture, and oil filters remove harmful metal shavings and other particles from the oil.

10. b. Mitigate between engine RPM (revolutions per minute) and wheel RPM
Car transmissions have many gears, switching between them as you increase or decrease in speed. Without a transmission, your wheels would turn precisely in relation to how fast the engine is going. At slow speeds, your engine would be turning slowly, and at high speeds, your engine would be screaming fast! The transmission allows the engine to maintain a reasonable RPM through the entire range of your car's capable speeds.

11. b. Cool the fluid that circulates the engine
Your car's engine burns hot, and if there were no way to cool it, the engine would completely and permanently fail. To prevent this, most car engines are cooled by a circulating mixture of water and radiator fluid. This concoction must be cooled as well, and that's where the radiator comes in. The radiator (usually located in the front of your engine compartment) is composed of a series of pipes and metal

fins. As you drive, air is forced past these fins, cooling the fluid before it circulates once more through the engine.

12. False

If you attach a tow rope directly to your bumper, you'll likely end up towing a bumper without your car! You need to attach the chain or cable directly to the car's chassis. To be sure you've got the right spot, consult your automotive manual.

BOATING

Believe me, my young friend; there is nothing —
absolutely nothing — half so much worth doing as
simply messing about in boats.

— KENNETH GRAHAME, *THE WIND IN THE WILLOWS* (1908)

1. Which side of a boat is the port?

a. Left

b. Right

2. Which side of a boat is the starboard?

a. Left

b. Right

3. Which end of a boat is the bow?

a. Front

b. Back

4. Which end of a boat is the stern?

a. Front

b. Back

5. Your boat has capsized, but remains floating upside down on the surface. You see another boat about a mile away, but no one on that boat appears to see you. What should you do?

a. Stay with your boat.

b. Swim toward the other boat.

c. Swim toward the other boat, keeping your disabled boat in sight.

6. You just turned your boat into a main channel but are not sure if you're heading toward or away from the ocean. The red channel markers are on your right. You are

a. Traveling away from the ocean

b. Traveling toward the ocean

THE ANSWER KEY

1. *a*. Left

Yes, it may sound ridiculous to have an alternate name for "left" or "right," but no one is going to change thousands of years of tradition to suit you! Even if you're simply boating recreationally in a small craft, expect your captain to use this and other nautical terms.

2. ♭. Right

Legend holds that the word starboard came from the Old English term "steorbord," meaning the "side of the ship that it's steered from." In olden times ships were steered with an oar near the back of the ship by a coxswain. Since most of these men were right-handed, they tended to stand and steer from the back right side of the ship.

3. *a*. Front

One legend holds that the term originated back when the bow of a boat was constructed from a bough of a large tree limb—a part of a tree that's exceptionally strong. The extra strength of the tree bough was ideal for the vulnerable front of the ship.

4. ♭. Back

Also called the "aft" part of a boat. The term "stern" originated from the part of a boat called a "sternpost"—an upright structural support post attached to the transom in the back of a wooden ship.

5. *a.* Stay with your boat.

Your only goal at this point is to be spotted by rescuers. Even the smallest boat creates a much larger visual "footprint" than a solitary man floating in a body of water. Further, distances on the water can be very deceiving—often appearing much closer than the reality. Even if another boat is nearby, currents might prevent you from getting there at all.

6. *a.* Traveling away from the ocean

Major waterways are marked with red and green markers placed on opposite sides of the channel. To determine which direction you're going in, remember the saying, "red right returning." If the red markers are on your right, you're returning from the sea.

URBAN AND OUTDOOR SURVIVAL

⁞⁞⁞

WHAT'S THE BEST way to survive an apartment fire? How about a plane crash? Or a flood, tornado, or hurricane? How can you prevent yourself from freezing to death in the open, or avoid drowning without the benefit of a life jacket? This chapter tests your ability to survive unexpected disasters, no matter where they happen.

19 OUTDOOR SURVIVAL

We all knew there was just one way to improve our odds for survival: train, train, train. Sometimes, if your training is properly intense, it will kill you. More often — much, much more often — it will save your life.

— RICHARD MARCINKO

1. A bear is about to attack. You should
   a. Run as fast as you can in the opposite direction
   b. Slowly back away, speaking softly, avoiding eye contact
   c. Stand tall, act aggressive, and shout at the bear
   d. Slowly back away, speak loudly, and stare the bear down

2. In spite of your actions, the bear attacks anyway. You should
   a. Free yourself, and run away as fast as you can
   b. Fight by targeting its eyes and neck
   c. Try to climb a nearby tree
   d. Lie face down, legs spread apart with your hands covering the back of your neck

3. Suddenly, and without warning, a shark attacks. What should you do?

   a. Repeatedly hit the shark on the snout.

   b. Don't try to fight, just swim away as fast as possible.

   c. Repeatedly jab your hand into the shark's gills and/ or eyes.

   d. Play dead.

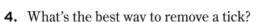

4. What's the best way to remove a tick?

   a. Apply alcohol, nail polish, or petroleum jelly to the tick and it will remove itself.

   b. Using tweezers, grasp the tick's body and pull out while twisting.

   c. Light a match, and touch the tick's body.

   d. Using tweezers, grasp the tick's body and pull out without twisting.

→ EDIBLE WILD PLANTS

Lost and starving in the wilderness? Take heart! You may just be trampling over your food source. Here are three widely available edible plants:

Cattails (technically *Typha latifolia*) are an excellent wild food source. Unlike most edible plants, there are parts of this plant that you can eat year round. Cattails grow in fresh water marshlands virtually all over the world—in North and South America, Asia, and parts of Europe. They can be

identified in late summer by the cigarlike seed heads at the top of the plant. In early spring, look for the cottony remnants of these and you'll know you've got the right plant. In the spring, the young shoots of the plant (the innermost part of the stem) can be eaten raw, and taste similar to cucumber. Steaming the shoots yields a cooked vegetable that tastes close to cabbage. In the summer, you can boil and eat the green male pollen spike, which has been compared in flavor to corn. During winter, the underground stems (rhizomes) are an excellent source of starch. Peel first, then work the starch out with your fingers into a large bowl of water. Let the starch settle, pour off the water, and then use the starch sediment to thicken a soup or broth.

The **common dandelion** may be considered a nuisance weed to most homeowners, but it's also an excellent edible plant. The best place to find them is in open, disturbed areas, e.g., between the edge of a road and the tree line. The young leaves and flowers can be eaten raw. Older leaves (and the roots) can be boiled and eaten as a cooked vegetable. Even the roots can be roasted and used as a coffee substitute.

The **prickly pear cactus** has been a food source for Mexico and Central America for thousands of years. It's also known as the paddle cactus due to its flat, paddle-like appearance. Although common in the deserts of the southwest, this wonderful food source can be found in seaside areas as far north as New York. All parts of the prickly pear are edible. However, you first must remove the cactus needles! To do so, lay the pads carefully over coals to burn off the spikes, or use a torch. Once the needles are removed, the pads can be either roasted or boiled as a vegetable—similar in texture to green beans. In late summer, the brightly colored blossoms (yellow, pink, red, or purple) ripen into a tasty red fruit. As with the paddles, remove the needles from the blossoms with a torch or over a fire. You can eat the fruits raw, or even make jams or pies as well.

A final word of caution. There are some poisonous plants that are similar in appearance to edible plants, so always be extra careful. Never attempt to eat *any* wild food unless you have positively identified it.

5. The following signs indicate that bad weather may be on the way:

   a. Geese flying high, high clouds, no wind

   b. Low clouds, geese flying low, swirling wind

c. Wolves howling, squirrels chirping, wispy clouds

d. Leaves falling, still winds, dropping temperatures

6. The best way to stay warm in cold weather is by using

a. Hand lotion

b. Multiple layers of clothing

c. Solid plastic outerwear

d. One thick garment

7. (True/False) You lose most of your body heat through your head.

8. The best way to pass a sharp knife to someone is to

a. Hold the knife gingerly by the point, and hand it over

b. Grasp the blade in your hand, with the sharp side facing out, then offer the handle

c. Hold half the handle with your fingers, then hand it so the person can grasp the other part of the handle

9. Which of the following knots is best to use for a critically important situation, e.g., lifting a person up from a well?

a. Granny knot

b. Figure 8 loop

c. Sheepshank

d. Bowline

10. You're caught in open water without a life jacket. How can you construct a makeshift life preserver out of your long pants?

    a. Blow into the pockets until they're filled with air, then grip the end of the pants and tie them around your neck.

    b. Tie a knot onto the end of each pant leg, grasp the waistband on either side with both hands, and fill the legs with air by rapidly moving the pants through the air. Place pants waist down into the water to create an air pocket.

    c. Put the pants on inside out and try to float with your feet much higher than your head, repeating as often as necessary.

11. You're camping and a terrible lightning storm erupts. How can you avoid being struck?

    a. Scrunch down in the open, away from your tent.

    b. Seek shelter in a shallow cave.

    c. Lie down in your tent.

    d. Scrunch down on your sleeping pad.

    e. Sit or lie at the base of a tree.

12. Which of the following combinations makes the best survival kit?

    a. Flint stick with wooden handle, piece of steel, large orange trash bag, whistle, and mirror

    b. Plastic Bic-type lighter, large orange trash bag, whistle, and mirror

    c. Flint stick with plastic handle, piece of steel, large orange trash bag, whistle, and mirror

13. You're caught in an avalanche. What's the best way to survive?

 a. "Swim" your way out of it, by using a freestyle swimming stroke to get to the surface.

 b. Attempt a series of leaps to propel yourself above the surface.

 c. Keep your hands close to your face while tumbling, and protrude one arm above the surface when the avalanche stops.

14. You're lost in the woods, no one knows you're there, and no one will likely report you missing. You have *no choice* but to try and get out. What should you do?

 a. Follow streams as they usually lead to civilization.

 b. Fix strips of cloth, clothing, etc., to a tree and mark a trail as you proceed.

 c. Wait till night time, and follow the North Star.

 d. Search for an open field and shout repeatedly.

15. You're lost, cold, and hungry, and it's starting to get dark. You should spend every available moment trying to:

 a. Locate food

 b. Locate suitable shelter

 c. Start a fire

16. The only water source available is from a stream or pond. Which of the following measures can you take to purify the water for drinking?

 a. Add 2 drops of bleach per quart, mix thoroughly.

b. Add 5 drops of iodine per quart, mix thoroughly.

c. Boil the water for at least 3 minutes, cool, then drink.

d. Any of the above.

17. You're lost in the woods, and it's starting to get very cold. The good news is that you remembered to bring pieces of flint and steel. Unfortunately, the kindling you were able to gather is damp. You come across an old garbage dump with the following items. Which one are you really glad to find?

a. Electric coffeemaker

b. Quart jar of sodium bicar-
bonate powder

c. Magnesium car wheel

d. 4 tubes of toothpaste

18. Which of the following should you remember before attempting to walk over a frozen pond or lake?

a. New ice is thicker than old ice, layers of snow slow the freezing process, and ice away from the shore is stronger.

b. Old ice is thicker than new ice, layers of snow speed the freezing process, and ice near the shore is stronger than ice further out.

THE ANSWER KEY

1. *b*. Slowly back away, speaking softly, avoiding eye contact

   Whatever you do, don't run! You'll only inspire him to chase you, and you can't outrun a bear.

2. *d*. Lie face down, legs spread apart with your hands covering the back of your neck

   By playing dead, you'll eventually make him lose interest in you and walk away.

3. *c*. Repeatedly jab your hand into the shark's gills and/or eyes.

   A shark's most sensitive places are the gills and eyes. Jab, poke, and grab these areas, and the shark may give up and seek easier prey.

4. *d*. Using tweezers, grasp the tick's body and pull out without twisting.

5. *b*. Low clouds, geese flying low, swirling wind

6. *b*. Multiple layers of clothing

7. False

   For some reason, this rumor has circulated for years!

8. ♭. Grasp the blade in your hand, with the sharp side facing out, then offer the handle.

9. ♭. Figure 8 loop

A rope is strongest when it has no knots, kinks, or loops. Every knot weakens the rope somewhat, usually between 20–40%. So when you're faced with a critical situation like having to lift someone from danger—you want to choose a knot that's reliable, easy to remember, and one that retains most of the rope's strength.

An ideal knot that's both strong and reliable is the figure 8 loop— so trustworthy that it's a major choice for rock climbers. It's a relatively easy knot to learn and remember, retains about 70–75% of the rope's strength, and is up to 15% stronger than a bowline. Here's how to tie one:

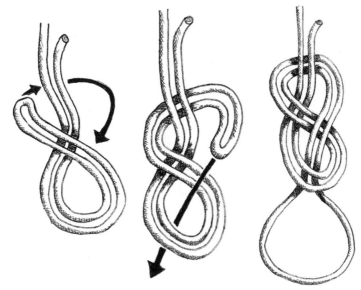

10. *b*. Tie a knot onto the end of each pant leg, grasp the waistband on either side with both hands, and fill the legs with air by rapidly moving the pants through the air. Place pants waist down into the water to create an air pocket.

11. *d*. Scrunch down on your sleeping pad.
You should also avoid

- *Other people—stay at least 20 feet apart*
- *Towers, bleachers, dug-outs, metal fences, and flagpoles*
- *Picnic and rain shelters (unless they have lightning protection arrestors)*
- *Any body of water, e.g., oceans, lakes, rivers, pools*
- *Convertible cars and golf carts*
- *Shallow caves*

12. *a*. Flint stick with wooden handle, piece of steel, large orange trash bag, whistle, and mirror
The reason that answer "A" is better than "C" is the wooden handle on the flint stick. In a pinch, you create kindling by scraping wooden shavings—a critical component for starting a fire—off the handle.

13. *a*. "Swim" your way out of it, by using a freestyle swimming stroke to get to the surface.

14. *b.* Fix strips of cloth, clothing, etc., to a tree and mark a trail as you proceed.

If for some reason, you get into an even worse position, e.g., low-lying swamps, precarious cliffs, etc., you'll always be able to find your way back by following your cloth strips.

15. *b.* Locate suitable shelter.

You can live three days without water, and three weeks without food, but being exposed to the elements, e.g. rain, snow, wind and/or cold (even temperatures well above freezing) can lead to hypothermia which can cause mental confusion, loss of consciousness and ultimately—death.

16. *d.* Any of the above

17. *c.* Magnesium car wheel

Magnesium shavings are extremely flammable and, therefore, an outstanding fire starter. Scrape shavings off the wheel with your piece of steel, pocket knife, etc., and then sprinkle them gingerly onto your kindling. Next, shower the magnesium pile with sparks by scraping your flint and steel together and voila!

18. *a.* New ice is thicker than old ice, layers of snow slow the freezing process, and ice away from the shore is stronger.

URBAN SURVIVAL

There are two big forces at work, external and internal. We have very little control over external forces such as tornadoes, earthquakes, floods, disasters, illness, and pain. What really matters is the internal force. How do I respond to those disasters?

— LEO BUSCAGLIA

1. (True/False) Your chances of surviving an airline crash improve 40% by sitting in the front of the plane.

2. In a hurricane, you're most likely to die from
    a. High winds and flying debris
    b. Government rescue efforts
    c. Inland flooding
    d. Starvation and/or dehydration

WHAT SHOULD YOU DO IF YOUR CAR VEERS OFF A BRIDGE?

If you stay in the car waiting for help to arrive, you better have your scuba gear on and ready—cars tend to sink *really* fast.

The weight of the engine will likely tilt the car nose forward as it takes on water. Despite your instincts to do otherwise, keep your seatbelt on initially. It keeps you oriented and gives you extra leverage. Try to open the door immediately upon hitting the water. Unless you do this before the water rises, the pressure of tons of water against your car will prevent you from doing so. If the car is tilting forward due to the engine weight, you may be able to open a rear door, if water has not yet reached the back. Your other best option is to get a window open fast. If the electric window motor or the hand crank won't work, bust the window out any way you can. Use a hammer or any heavy object, hit up against it with your shoulder, or brace yourself and kick it out. If, in spite of your efforts, you're still unable to get the window open, wait until the car is totally filled with water and then try opening the doors.

3. You're driving on a highway, and a tornado is bearing down on you. It's too close to escape. What's the best way to survive?

   a. Seek shelter under a highway overpass.

   b. Find a (dry) low area, lie face down with your hands protecting the back of your head.

   c. Stay in your vehicle, buckle your seat belt (if not buckled already), and try to drive at right angles to the storm movement and out of the path of the tornado.

4. For wood, paper, or cloth fires, use a Class _____ fire extinguisher to douse the flames.

   a. A

   b. B

   c. C

   d. D

   e. K

5. Which method(s) are appropriate for extinguishing a stove-top grease fire?

   a. Put a lid over the pan to cover it completely, and turn off the heat.

   b. Douse the fire with a pan full of water.

   c. Throw baking soda over the flames.

   d. Use a Class B fire extinguisher.

6. (True/False) Most victims of fires die from smoke or toxic gases and not from burns.

THE ANSWER KEY

1. False

   About 95% of airplane crashes have survivors, and according to the magazine Popular Mechanics, *you're 40% more likely to survive if you're sitting in the back of the plane.*

2. *c.* Inland flooding

   Flying debris from high winds can be deadly. Government rescue efforts can be comical, but they rarely lead to serious injury. Flooding, on the other hand, causes more deaths than anything else in a hurricane.

3. *c.* Stay in your vehicle, buckle your seat belt (if not buckled already), and try to drive at right angles to the storm movement and out of the path of the tornado.

4. *a.* A

   Use the wrong type of extinguisher, and you may actually make the situation worse.

CLASS:	EXTINGUISHES:
A	Ordinary combustible items such as wood, most plastics, paper, cloth, cardboard, etc.
B	Flammable or combustible liquids like grease, alcohol, oil, or gasoline
C	Anything electric, such as outlets, appliances, or circuit breakers
D	Commercial applications with specialized fires
K	Commercial applications with specialized fires

5. *a, c, d.* Put a lid over the pan to cover it completely and turn off the heat; Throw baking soda over the flames; Use a Class B fire extinguisher.

The last thing you want to do is to try and put out a grease fire with water—for you're only going to spread the flames.

6. True

According to the Centers for Disease Control and Prevention, you're more likely to die from asphyxiation (impairment of normal breathing due to inhalation of toxic gases and/or smoke) than from burns. Increase your chances of survival by having smoke alarms in operating condition (4 out of 10 deaths are in homes without them).

SELF-DEFENSE

The purpose of fighting is to win. There is no possible victory in defense. The sword is more important than the shield and skill is more important than either. The final weapon is the brain. All else is supplemental.

—JOHN STEINBECK

If at all possible, you should always avoid confrontation. You may end up in a situation, however, where you have no choice but to defend yourself. You might also be faced with a confrontation where you have to protect a close friend or relative. Either way, knowing self-defense techniques may help you avoid injury or even save your—or a loved one's—life.

1. (True/False) You're under attack suddenly and people are near-by. The best way to get their attention is to yell the word "Help!"

2. (True/False) An attacker has you from behind with his hands around your neck. The best way to get him to release you is to grasp his hands and yank them away from your neck.

3. (True/False) Before punching someone, tense your muscles and clench your fist early to enhance the power of your blow.

4. (True/False) When you're absolutely certain you're about to be attacked, strike your opponent first.

5. (True/False) Using your teeth is largely ineffective against a determined attacker.

6. The *SAS Self-Defense Handbook* recommends that you carry which of the following for your safety?
   a. Loaded handgun
   b. Ball point pen
   c. Sharp knife
   d. Newspaper
   e. Stun gun

THE ANSWER KEY

1. False

Yelling the word "help" may not have any impact, as people joking around often shout the word without really meaning it. Instead, try yelling "CALL 911," followed immediately with the reason and a description of the attacker, e.g., "I'm being attacked by two heavyset men with beards!"

2. False

A better technique is to make a "V" with your arms by clasping your hands together and then thrust them upward—forcing his arms, and his grasp away from your neck.

3. False

The late famous martial arts expert Bruce Lee put it this way: "Relaxation is essential for faster and more powerful punching. Let your lead punch shoot out loosely and easily; do not tighten up or clench your fist until the moment of impact."

4. True

By striking him first, you may lessen his ability to fight back—and he may even give up before he starts.

5. False

Biting can be an extremely effective defense, as it can inflict an extreme amount of pain—perhaps disabling your attacker. If close enough, try for an ear. If he attacks with his hands, bite fingers, the palm, or forearm. Don't let go! Hang on and tear the flesh.

6. b, d. Ball point pen; Newspaper

DOMESTIC SKILLS

||||||||||||||||||||||||||||||||||||||||||||||||||||||||||||||||||||||||||||||||||||||

DO YOU HAVE a personal chef, a gardener, and several servants to take care of your household needs? If not, then the burdens of feeding, clothing, cleaning, and house maintenance fall directly on you. Whether or not you become an accomplished chef—or simply learn how to fry a hamburger—you absolutely need to understand basic food safety. If not, you may spend an agonizing night in an emergency room with excruciating symptoms.

How about proper grooming? This may seem like a topic that's more appropriate for women, but a poorly groomed man might find himself *without* the company of women. And what about cleaning your clothes and maintaining the condition of your apartment or home? Improper clothes cleaning can quickly ruin your wardrobe, and even new dwellings require basic maintenance (an expensive ordeal if you have to hire someone—rather than doing it yourself). The following section tests your skills and offers tips in the domestic arena.

GROOMING

You are your greatest asset. Put your time, effort, and money into training, grooming, and encouraging your greatest asset.

—TOM HOPKINS, AUTHOR AND SALES TRAINER

1. If you have a round face, which of the following hairstyles should you avoid?

   a. Very short hairstyle cropped close to the scalp

   b. Hairstyles that add mass or volume to the sides

   c. Short hairstyles with height on top, like a "faux hawk"

   d. Hairstyles that hang over onto your face or eyes

→ WHAT'S YOUR FACE SHAPE?

Everyone's face can be categorized into one of seven different shapes: oval, round, oblong, diamond, down-triangle (wide at top), up-triangle (wide at bottom), and square, and each shape requires different hairstyles. According to the website www.coolmenshair.com, choosing the right hairstyle is important because it helps minimize less-attractive features.

Take a look in the mirror to determine which type you resemble most closely. If you have a round face, you want to choose

ROUND   **SQUARE**

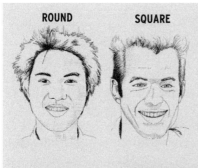

UP-TRIANGLE   **DOWN-TRIANGLE**

DIAMOND   **OBLONG**

OVAL

a hairstyle that minimizes the width of your face. Choose cuts that are narrow on the sides, and higher on the top. Avoid full hair styles as they emphasize the roundness of your face. Similarly, square faces require less width on the sides and more height on top. If you have a long face, choose styles with less weight on the top and more length on the sides. If you have an up-triangle face, choose styles that give the illusion of widening your forehead. With a down-triangle, choose styles that do the opposite. With diamond-shaped faces, the goal is to minimize your wide cheekbones and to balance your narrow forehead and chin. Choose styles with bangs and/or longer hair. If you have an oblong face, choose short- to medium-length hairstyles, with bangs over your forehead. This should help your face appear shorter and broader. Do you have an oval face? Consider yourself fortunate, as most hairstyles look good on you.

2. (True/False) If you have an oval-shaped face, you can choose almost any beard style and look good.

3. If you have a square face, choose these types of glasses:
   a. Frames with thin rims, that are wider at the bottom
   b. Frames with more width and less depth
   c. Rimless, semi-rimless oval, or cat's-eye shapes

4. (True/False) Only a small minority of women think that the presence of back hair on a man is unattractive.

5. When shaving with a razor, it's best to shave ____ the grain of your beard.
   a. With
   b. Against
   c. Sideways
   d. Doesn't matter

According to the health website WebMD.com, "The average man has more than 25,000 hairs as hard as copper wire coming out of his face and spends 3,000 hours in his lifetime shaving them off."

6. When using an electric shaver, it's best to shave _____ the grain of your beard.

    a. With

    b. Against

    c. Sideways

    d. Doesn't matter

7. About _____% of girls said that a guy's skin is very important to them and that they like touchable skin.

    a. 5

    b. 25

    c. 55

    d. 75

→ FOUR STEPS TO SMOOTHER SKIN

How can you attain skin that's more touchable? Follow this four-step process:

1. Cleanse
2. Exfoliate
3. Moisturize
4. Sunscreen

Soap is typically okay for anything below the neck, but purchase a facial cleanser that's strong enough to get rid of grease, yet mild enough to be used every day. Next, exfoliate (a fancy term for "peeling off a thin layer of dead skin") three times a week. Exfoliating goes further than normal cleansing as it unclogs pores and eliminates excess dirt buildup. Through the act of shaving, men naturally exfoliate parts of their face, but you should also use an exfoliating cream. Choose one with tiny scrubbing granules (as larger grains tend to tear up your skin). Then, apply a moisturizer. Moisturizers replenish your skin's moisture which is robbed by sun, wind, soaps, and chemicals like pool chlorine. Dry skin is not only less touchable, but it also leads to wrinkles and premature skin aging. Finally, help to eliminate the number one cause of wrinkles (sun damage) by applying a broad-spectrum sunscreen (protects against both UVA and UVB rays).

THE ANSWER KEY

1. ♭. Hairstyles that add mass or volume to the sides

If you have a round face, you want to choose a hairstyle that minimizes the width of your face. Choose cuts that are narrow on the sides, and higher on the top.

2. True

If you have an oval shaped face, you're in luck. Virtually any beard style should look good on you. If you have a round or square face, choose longer beard styles to minimize the roundness of your face and make your head appear longer.

3. ♭. Frames with more width and less depth

If you have a square face with a strong jaw line, you'll want to diminish your angles. Try frames with soft curves or ovals, and frames that have less height and more width. For oblong faces, choose frames with less width, more depth. Make sure the frames aren't any wider than the widest part of your face.

4. False

According to a grooming survey by the Remington Corporation, more than 70% of women prefer men to trim their back hair, and a third of women prefer a completely shaven back. Don't forget nose and ear hair. About half the women surveyed find it troublesome when men fail to keep these areas trimmed.

5. *a.* With

Not doing so may cause razor burn.

6. *b.* Against

As with a blade, it's best to soften your facial hair and open facial pores before shaving. Try shaving right after a hot shower, or alternately, drape a warm washcloth over your face for a minute before beginning. Dry your face thoroughly first, and consider using an alcohol-based pre-shave (if your skin is not too sensitive). The alcohol will help to dry your skin prior to shaving.

7. *d.* 75

CLOTHING

With a poorly dressed man, you notice the clothes; with a well-dressed man, you notice the man.

— ANONYMOUS

You only have a few seconds to make a first impression, and your clothes play a major factor. This doesn't mean that you need to dress in business suits all of the time. The right T-shirt and jeans can make the right statement in the proper situation. Choose your clothing carefully and you'll enhance your image. Wear the wrong styles and colors, however, and you may create a poor impression before you even open your mouth.

1. (True/False) Your belt color should match the color of your shoes.

2. In general, black shoes work best with which color pants?
   a. Gray, black, navy
   b. Beige, brown, tan, greens, dark earth tones

3. (True/False) If you're skinny, you should wear vertically striped shirts to help broaden your appearance.

4. (True/False) If you're particularly hefty around the middle, avoid heavy fabrics like tweeds and thick wool suits.

5. If you're short (5' 6" or under), which three of the following should you avoid?
   a. Pants with cuffs
   b. Thin-knot ties
   c. Dark colors
   d. Long suit jackets
   e. Loud patterns
   f. Pinstripes

6. If you have a flat butt, it's best to choose pants that
   a. Are loose in the rear
   b. Are tighter in the rear
   c. Hang low

7. If you're tall (6' 2" or over), which four of the following should you employ in your clothing choices?

a. Suspenders

b. Separate colors for jacket/pants

c. Pointy collars

d. Wider ties

e. Large pant cuffs

f. Horizontal stripes

THE ANSWER KEY

1. True

Unless your belt is made up of many colors—which is a style you probably should avoid!

2. *a.* Grey, black, navy

Brown shoes go best with beige, brown, tan, greens, and dark earth tone pants. What if you have burgundy colored shoes? Pair them with lighter brown, khaki, and even blue and gray pants.

3. False

Vertical stripes actually make you appear thinner—a great choice if you're a heavyset person. Try horizontal stripes if you're skinny and you want to appear larger—but stay away from them if you're wide in the middle, as they'll make you appear even bigger. In the same way, large patterns (e.g., plaids) make you appear bigger, while smaller patterns do the opposite.

4. True

5. *a, d, e.* Pants with cuffs; Long suit jackets; Loud patterns

Thin-knot ties, vertical stripes (e.g., pinstripes), pointed collar shirts, and darker colors may help you to appear a bit taller. Avoid oversized garments, and pants that are too long, and consider using

suspenders instead of a belt (the waist line is raised and the eye is drawn in a vertical direction).

6. ♭. Are tighter in the rear

To accent the most of what you do have, you can also draw more attention to your backside by wearing shorter jackets that don't drop past the waist, and select fuller shirts that are fitted at the waist.

7. ♭, d, e, f. Separate colors for jacket/pants; Wider ties; Large pant cuffs; Horizontal stripes

Suspenders make men look taller, so tall men should stick with belts. Separate colors for suit jackets and pants is a good idea, as they break up the tall appearance. Choose spread collars, rather than pointy, as pointed collars draw the eye vertically. Slightly wider ties, horizontal stripes, pleated trousers, and larger pant cuffs also help to "shorten" a man.

THE KITCHEN

One of the very nicest things about life is the way we must regularly stop whatever it is we are doing and devote our attention to eating.

— LUCIANO PAVAROTTI AND WILLIAM WRIGHT,
PAVAROTTI: MY OWN STORY

1. According to the United States Department of Agriculture what's the recommended minimum internal cooked temperature for beef, lamb, and veal roasts so they're safe to eat?

   a. 120°F

   b. 145°F

   c. 195°F

   d. 290°F

2. (True/False) If an egg sinks in a bowl of water, it may be spoiled.

3. (True/False) If you get sick, it's always from the last food you ate.

4. What's the recommended minimum internal cooked temperature that *ground* beef, lamb, or veal should be so they're safe to eat?

a. 120°F

b. 145°F

c. 160°F

d. 290°F

5. (True/False) You're more likely to accidentally cut yourself with a dull knife rather than a sharp one.

6. According to the United States Department of Agriculture, your refrigerator should be set to a minimum of ____.

a. 20°F

b. 32°F

c. 40°F

d. 49°F

A freezer's job (set at 0°F or below) is to *stop* the growth of bacteria by halting their growth entirely. Ideally, we'd freeze everything, but many foods don't freeze well (e.g., eggs, lettuce), and it's not practical to thaw everything at the time when you need it, like something to drink.

7. (True/False) If the hamburger you're grilling is brown in the middle, it's a good indicator that it is now safe to eat.

8. (True/False) When someone gets sick from potato salad that was left out too long, it's probably the mayonnaise that spoiled.

Why be concerned with the proper handling and cooking of foods? The Centers for Disease Control in Atlanta reports that contaminated foods cause 76 million illnesses, 300,000 hospitalizations, and 5,000 deaths in the United States each year. Food poisoning usually involves feeling sick to your stomach, vomiting, stomach cramps, and continuous diarrhea. Not a great way to spend two to three days of your time!

Food poisoning is most often caused by parasites, viruses, and bacteria—usually found in raw meats, fish, and eggs (or on other foods that have been cross-contaminated by these). Animals naturally have bacteria in their intestines, but the danger occurs when this bacteria gets inadvertently mixed into the other edible parts of the animals we eat. You can also get these harmful organisms from food handlers who neglected to wash their hands or from food that's begun to spoil from sitting out of the refrigerator too long. You can't always tell if a food is bad from visual observation, tasting, or smelling. In fact, tasting a food to see if it's bad is never recommended as less than 10 bacteria (e.g., *E. coli*) can cause a food-borne illness. Consider this too: in food left at room temperature, 1 bacterium can multiply to 2,095,152 in just seven hours!

9. (True/False) For proper food safety, it's *not* recommended to wash meats and poultry prior to cooking.

10. (True/False) Canned foods can be kept indefinitely, as long as the can is not damaged.

THE ANSWER KEY

1. *b*. 145°F

All cuts of pork should be cooked to a minimum of 160°F.

2. False

If an egg floats in a bowl of water, it just may be spoiled. Eggs naturally contain a small air pocket that enlarges over time, but there's initially not enough air for an egg to float. Eventually, the air cell increases to a point where an egg may become buoyant. Eggs that float are certainly old, but they may still be okay to eat. The ultimate test is to crack the egg into a bowl and check for unusual color and/or unpleasant odors. If either is present, it's probably best not to eat it.

3. False

It can take from half an hour up until six weeks to become ill from something you ate.

4. *c*. 160°F

Why is there a cooking temperature difference between roasts and ground meats? The process of grinding meats increases the chance of exposure to harmful bacteria. You reduce your risks of contracting food poisoning by cooking the meat to a higher temperature.

5. True

When trying to cut slick objects like onions or apples, a dull knife may deflect and slip off the surface, rather than cutting into it, and is more likely to cause an accident. On the other hand, a sharp knife will more easily cut a food when you apply pressure—giving you greater control over your cutting task.

6. *c.* 40°F

7. False

The only way to determine whether your hamburger has been cooked to the right temperature (160 degrees) is through the use of a meat thermometer.

8. False

Actually, mayonnaise is probably the safest ingredient in potato salad—and the least likely to spoil. If the potato salad goes bad, the potatoes or eggs are the likely culprits. Germs can easily grow in either if they are not kept cold.

9. True

Washing only increases the chances for spreading bacteria (cross-contamination) to other foods, kitchen surfaces, and cooking utensils.

10. False

If the can remains in good condition—no dents, rust, etc.—then low-acid foods (meats, fish, and most vegetables) can be retained for up to five years. On the other hand, high-acid foods, such as grapefruit, tomatoes, cranberries, and pineapple, should be stored for less than 18 months.

LAUNDRY AND IRONING

I see TV ads about detergents that can get blood stains out of your clothes. I say if you have blood stains on your clothes you should be thinking about something other than laundry.

—JERRY SEINFELD

1. (True/False) There's no need to separately wash your white and colored clothes as long as you use the warm water setting on your washing machine.

2. (True/False) Using the hot water setting in your washer kills all germs in your wash load.

3. (True/False) If you're getting an unusually large amount of lint in your dryer's lint trap, then you're probably using too much detergent.

4. Your iron's temperature settings from coolest to warmest are
   a. Wool, cotton, silk
   b. Silk, wool, cotton
   c. Cotton, silk, wool

5. (True/False) If some of your clothes have been shrinking, it's primarily caused by a lack of moisture, and not high dryer heat.

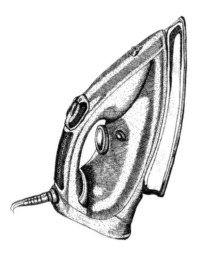

6. It's best to fill your iron with _____ water, rather than tap water.

  a. Distilled

  b. Mineral

  c. Vitamin-fortified

7. (True/False) When trying to remove stains like blood, wine, or coffee, it's recommended you wash clothes in cold water.

→ LAUNDRY 101

At the very least sort your clothes into whites (and light colors), and darker colors. First, check the tags on your clothes for the care instructions. If any state "Dry clean only," take them to the cleaners instead. See if the tags recommend a washing temperature, and sort accordingly. Next, check your pockets! Nothing can ruin your clothes faster than a ballpoint pen leaking all over your wash load.

Once sorted, spray any stains with a laundry pre-treatment product. Pick some up at the grocery store in the laundry products aisle. Choose hot water for your whites/light colors, and if you want some extra cleaning power, add bleach to your load in addition to the laundry soap. Once the clothes are thoroughly mixed with water and detergent, pour 1 cup of bleach (for large loads) into the washer. Alternately, pour the bleach into the appropriate dispenser (if the machine has one). For colored clothes, pre-treat stains and choose the cold water setting on your washing machine. Forget using bleach though, as it may permanently remove fabric colors.

THE ANSWER KEY

1. False

You wash white clothes separately because you want them to stay white. If you mix colors with whites, the dyes from the colored clothes may bleed onto your whites and lighter colored clothes.

2. False

The only way to effectively kill germs and sanitize your washer is by adding chlorine bleach to your wash load.

3. True

If you're getting an unusually large amount of lint in your dryer's lint trap, then you're probably using too much detergent.

4. b. Silk, wool, cotton

Make sure you use the right temperature setting, or you may scorch your clothes!

5. True

A common myth is that high dryer heat shrinks clothes. The real culprit, however, is lack of moisture, which can happen if you over-dry your clothes. To prevent the risk of shrinking them, pull your clothes out of the dryer while still damp.

6. *a.* Distilled

Tap water contains various amounts of minerals and when the water is turned to steam in the iron, these minerals are expelled in solid form (sometimes a whitish powder). This residue will not only clog your iron over time, but it also may be ironed on to your clothes, creating unsightly, powdery stains. You can find distilled water at the grocery store.

7. True

Hot water may actually set blood, wine, or coffee stains—making the blemish permanent.

HOME MAINTENANCE

EVEN BRAND NEW homes are prone to problems—and if you have an older residence, be prepared for constant maintenance challenges. You can always call an electrician, plumber, or general repairman, but with a little knowledge, you can save thousands of dollars a year by fixing things yourself.

PLUMBING

A man builds a fine house; and now he has a master, and a task for life: he is to furnish, watch, show it, and keep it in repair, the rest of his days.

— RALPH WALDO EMERSON

1. Which of the following is a function of the elbow trap in a sink drain?
   a. To create a clog area that's convenient to clean
   b. To drain the sink at a consistent rate
   c. To prevent water from backing up into the sink

2. Which of the following methods may be used to clear a drain if you have PVC pipes connected to your sink?
   a. Boiling water
   b. Plunger
   c. Drum auger

3. Before installing a new showerhead, wrap ____ tape around the pipe threads to prevent leaks.

a. Electrical

b. Duct

c. Teflon

d. Scotch

4. (True/False) Under no circumstances should you attempt to unclog a toilet by inserting a coat hanger into the bowl drain.

THE ANSWER KEY

1. *a.* To create a clog area that's convenient to clean.

In spite of our best efforts, a lot of insoluble junk, such as hair, dirt, and personal items, finds its way into our sink drains. Without an elbow trap (also known as a J-bend), this waste would eventually form a clog somewhere in your pipes. Rather than having to tear down half your house in search of an elusive clog, the elbow trap is designed as kind of a catchall to collect this debris. Another function of the J-bend is to prevent sewer gases from entering your home. It's conveniently located directly under your sink, so it can be removed and cleaned easily.

2. *b, c.* Plunger; Drum auger

While it can be a good idea to clear clogs with boiling water in sinks equipped with metal pipes, you don't want to try this with pipes made of PVC. PVC (polyvinyl chloride) is a type of plastic—one that tends to melt at about 175°F.

3. *c.* Teflon

4. False

A coat hanger can be a great tool for unclogging a toilet if you don't have an auger handy. Untwist the hanger to form a straight wire. Insert one end deep into the toilet bowl, then turn the wire both clockwise and then counterclockwise while moving the wire in and out. If you're pulling up any material on the end of the wire, you're probably making progress. Continue until the toilet flushes freely.

ELECTRICAL

Electricity is really just organized lightning.

— GEORGE CARLIN, COMEDIAN

Note: Working with electricity can be both risky and very dangerous. Before attempting any electrical wiring, turn off the power at your home's main circuit breaker.

1. Electric outlet boxes in your home will likely contain these three types of wires:
   a. A hot (black), a cold, and a yellow
   b. A hot (black), a neutral (white), and a ground
   c. A cold, a neutral (white), and a ground
   d. A ground, a warm (blue), and a hot (black)

2. When attaching wires in a wall box for electric plugs, follow this rule:
   a. Attach the neutrals (white) wire to the two side screws that are on the *same* side as the ground (green or bare wire) screw. The hots (black) will attach to the remaining two screws.

b. Attach the neutrals (white) to the two side screws that are on the *opposite* side as the ground (green or bare wire) screw. The hots (black) will attach to the remaining two screws.

c. Either of the above is correct.

3. A GFCI circuit stands for
   a. Google Facebook Cooperating Internet
   b. Greatest Fool Communication Initiative
   c. Gold Fence Classic Interrogation
   d. Ground Fault Circuit Interrupter

1. ♭. A hot (black), a neutral (white), and a ground

To help in understanding wiring, household electric cables are color-coded. The hot wire (black) supplies the current, while the neutral wire (white or gray) carries it back to complete the circuit. The ground wire (green or bare) is there for a kind of insurance. If you have a malfunction in the electric outlet box, a lamp, ceiling fan, power tool, etc., the ground wire carries the current back so you don't get shocked.

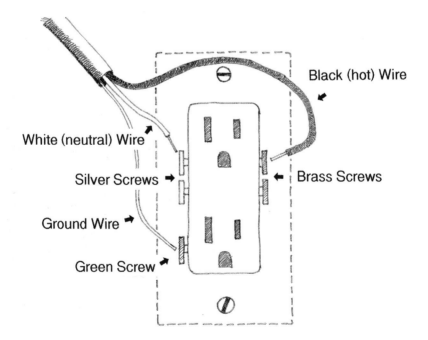

Black (hot) Wire

White (neutral) Wire

Silver Screws ➡

Brass Screws ⬅

Ground Wire ➡

Green Screw ➡

2. *a.*

Outlets and plugs are polarized, meaning that you can insert a plug only one way (note that one outlet slot—the neutral—is taller than the other). To insure that your outlet is wired correctly, you need to attach the neutral (white or gray) wires to the two side screws on the same side as the ground (green or bare wire). Attach the hot (black) wires to the other side.

3. *d.* Ground Fault Circuit Interrupter

Electric shocks can occur when your hand (or other body part) provides a path between an electric source and a ground. A GFCI (ground fault circuit interrupter) is an electrical device designed to prevent you from getting a severe shock when this electric "leak" occurs. Some GFCIs are installed directly in your home's main circuit panel, but more commonly you'll see them built into receptacles in your bathroom, kitchen, garage, and outside.

28

GENERAL

One only needs two tools in life: WD-40 to make things go, and duct tape to make them stop.

— G.M. WEILACHER

1. What's the significance of the "frost line" in home building?
   a. It's the depth in the exterior wall where freezing air can penetrate.
   b. It's the maximum depth groundwater in soil is expected to freeze.
   c. It's the distance from the sides of the house where frost can be expected.

2. At what temperature should your water heater be set?
   a. 120°F
   b. 140°F
   c. 180°F
   d. 212°F

3. What's the purpose of attic vents?

    a. To reduce attic temperature swings

    b. To extend the life of asphalt shingles

    c. To reduce moisture in attics

    d. All of the above

4. (True/False) Furnace filters should be replaced once each season.

THE ANSWER KEY

1. *b*. It's the maximum depth groundwater in soil is expected to freeze. *When water freezes, it expands—often exerting tremendous force. This force can literally shift the foundation of a building, bridge, or fence posts—a process known as frost heave. Therefore, it's critical to establish the depth of these foundations below the point in the soil where water could be expected to freeze—also known as the frost line. Clearly, the frost line depth can be quite different depending on where you live. In Florida, for example, there is no established frost line, yet in places like northern Michigan, the frost line is 60 inches down.*

2. *a*. 120°F
   Water set to only 5 degrees higher than this can cause second or third degree burns to a child after just 2 minutes of exposure. Annually, nearly 4,000 people in the United States are injured and more than 30 people die from scalding by excessively hot tap water in the home.

3. *d*. All of the above

4. False
   Furnace filters should be changed as often as needed—sometimes several times per heating or cooling season.

PAINTING

If bad decorating was a hanging offense, there'd be bodies hanging from every tree!

— SYLVESTER STALLONE

1. Painting a room with a darker color will
   a. Make the room appear smaller
   b. Make the room appear taller
   c. Make the room appear larger

2. (True/False) When painting an interior room, you should choose high-gloss paint for the trim areas (moldings, window frame, door frames, etc.) and flat-finish paints for the walls and ceilings.

3. (True/False) The advantages of oil-based (alkyd) over latex paints are that they dry faster, and allow you to clean your brushes with soap and water.

THE ANSWER KEY

1. *a*. Make the room appear smaller

Conversely, painting rooms with lighter colors makes them appear bigger.

2. True

Flat paint has little or no shine to it, while gloss paints (semi or high) have a shiny finish. Higher-gloss finishes are used on trim areas as they are both durable and washable. Handprints are more likely to be found on door and window frames, and therefore you want an easy-to-clean painting surface on these areas. Flat finishes are best suited for regions that receive less wear, like the walls or ceiling in a room.

3. False

Latex paints usually dry to the touch in about 30 minutes, while alkyd paints (formerly known as oil-based paints) take 4 to 6 hours. Further, paint brushes used with latex paints can be cleaned with soap and water, while alkyd paints require a paint solvent. Then, why even bother with alkyd paints? While latex is used most often, alkyd paints have a smoother, harder finish, and are better suited for metal surfaces. They also dry virtually free of brush marks.

HEALTH, NUTRITION, AND LIFESTYLE

||||||||||||||||||||||||||||||||||||||||||||||||||||||||||||||||||||

WHEN WE'RE YOUNG, we take good health for granted. I look good and feel healthy, so what's another greasy cheeseburger going to hurt? Why worry about too much sugar or a bunch of calories? Why bother with exercise? Because—the habits (bad or good) we adopt in our youth set the stage for our personal health for the rest of our lives.

With the right diet, exercise, and a healthy lifestyle, you have a greater chance of living a long life of happiness. With the *wrong* diet, and little or no exercise, however, you might fall considerably short of the national life expectancy for men of 77.4 years.

Do you know the correct choices for leading and maintaining a healthy lifestyle? If you want to stay healthy—you'll need this critical information.

NUTRITION

Without health life is not life; it is only a state of languor and suffering—an image of death.

— BUDDHA

1. Fats tend to get a bad rap. However, not all fats are bad. Which two of the following are considered good fats?

   a. Monounsaturated fats

   b. Trans fats

   c. Saturated fats

   d. Polyunsaturated fats

2. Approximately how many calories should a moderately active 19–30-year-old man consume each day?

   a. 600–900

   b. 2,100–2,400

   c. 2,600–2,800

   d. 4,400–5,000

   e. 11,500–14,000

3. Federal nutrition guidelines state that fats should be ____% of your daily caloric intake.

  a. less than 10

  b. 10–20

  c. 20–35

  d. 35–60

4. As part of a healthy diet, a man 19–50 years old should consume approximately ____ per day.

  a. 1 cup of fruit and 1/2 cup of vegetables

  b. 2 cups of fruit and 3 cups of vegetables

  c. 3 cups of fruit and 3 cups of vegetables

5. (True/False) Many *frozen* fruits and vegetables are typically more nutritious than the fresh selections found in your supermarket.

6. Teenagers and young adults (who are not lactose-sensitive) require about ____ cup(s) of milk or equivalent dairy products per day.

  a. ½

  b. 1

  c. 2

  d. 3

7. Federal nutrition guidelines state that you should consume less than ___ mg of sodium (salt) per day.

   a. 2,300 (approximately 1 tsp. of salt)

   b. 4,600 (approximately 2 tsp. of salt)

   c. 6,900 (approximately 3 tsp. of salt)

   d. 14,335 (approximately 6 tsp. of salt)

8. Teenage boys and men need about ___ grams of protein each day.

   a. 12–16

   b. 52–56

   c. 122–166

   d. 175–300

THE ANSWER KEY

1. **a, d.** Monounsaturated fats; Polyunsaturated fats
   Bad fats (trans and saturated) can elevate the cholesterol levels in the blood, increasing your risk of coronary heart disease. Good fats, on the other hand, actually lower cholesterol in the blood.

2. **c.** 2,600–2,800
   As a point of reference, McDonald's Egg and Cheese McGriddles have 560 calories. A Wendy's Triple Hamburger with Cheese has 1,030 calories, more than one third of the recommended calorie intake all by itself.

3. **c.** 20–35

4. **b.** 2 cups of fruit and 3 cups of vegetables
   Yes, a large sirloin steak can fill you up all by itself, but fruits and vegetables are extremely important for your overall nutrition. The Centers for Disease Control and Prevention states that "Fruits and vegetables contain essential vitamins, minerals, and fiber that may help protect you from chronic diseases."

5. **True**
   Crops destined to be frozen are picked at their height of ripeness, as they are usually processed and frozen right away. Fresh vegetables

and fruits destined for your supermarket are usually picked well before reaching their peak, as they have to last during both shipping and the display time.

6. *d.* 3

Don't like milk? An equivalent dairy serving is 1 1/2 ounces of natural (not processed) cheese, or 1 cup of yogurt. Dairy products are important sources of calcium, potassium, vitamin D, and protein—critical components for maintaining good health, bones, and teeth.

7. *a.* 2,300 (approximately 1 tsp. of salt)

Salt helps to maintain the body's balance of fluids. However, nearly all of us ingest more salt than we need. But, you say, "I hardly ever pick up the salt shaker!" By far, the largest percentage of salt intake—75%—comes from salt added to processed foods by manufacturers or at restaurants. It may be difficult to determine the salt content of foods you order at restaurants, but always read the food label on packaged foods. Anything containing 5% or less of the recommended daily intake is considered low sodium, anything above 20% is considered high.

8. *b.* 52–56

A 4 oz. hamburger patty contains about 28 grams and a 3.5 oz. chicken breast has about 30 grams.

31

FIRST AID

Know safety, no injury. No safety, know injury.

— ANONYMOUS

1. You've been stung by a bee. You're not having a full-blown allergic reaction, but the sting area is starting to itch. Thankfully, you have some of this with you:

   a. Sudafed

   b. Benadryl

   c. Guaifenesin

   d. Tums

2. Doctors recommend getting a tetanus shot every ____ years.

   a. 2

   b. 5

   c. 10

   d. 15

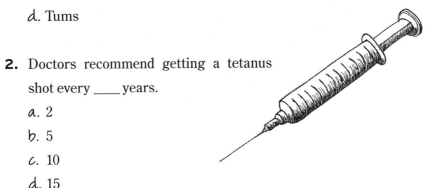

3. (True/False) It's always best to puncture a blister, rather than keeping it intact.

4. The best treatment for minor burns is to

    a. Hold an ice pack against the burn

    b. Run cool water over the burn

    c. Apply an ointment or butter to the burn

    d. All of the above

A first-degree burn is one where only the outer layer of skin is burned. The burned area is painful, red, and may involve swelling. A second-degree burn is where both the outer layer and inner layer of skin are burned. The area will be red, painful, swollen, and have blistering. Third-degree burns (the most serious) cause permanent tissue damage and involve all layers of the skin. They may also affect bone and muscles. These burns are characterized by white or charred black skin.

---

5. (True/False) You're confronted with someone who has severe, third-degree burns (his exposed skin is charred black and parts may be ashen white). You should immediately remove the scorched clothing near his burns while waiting for help to arrive.

6. A person you're with is beginning to have a heart attack. After immediately calling 911, you should give him ____.

    a. An ibuprofen tablet

    b. A regular-sized aspirin

    c. Some parsley

    d. An allergy tablet

HOW DO YOU KNOW IF SOMEONE'S HAVING A HEART ATTACK?

Here are some symptoms to watch out for:
- Fainting, light-headedness, or nausea
- Pain in the arms, shoulders, neck, jaw, back or stomach area
- Numbness or tingling—usually in the left arm
- Pressure, pain, or "fullness" in the center of the chest that lasts for more than just a few minutes

7. To take care of a small wound, it's best to do the following:
   a. Clean the wound with cool water and a mild soap, apply a thin layer of antibiotic cream, cover with a bandage.
   b. Clean the wound with cool water and a mild soap, apply iodine or hydrogen peroxide, cover with a bandage.
   c. Clean the wound with cool water and a mild soap, apply iodine or hydrogen peroxide and a thin layer of antibiotic cream, cover with a bandage.

→ HOW TO PERFORM THE HEIMLICH MANEUVER

1. If the person is conscious, position yourself behind the victim and wrap your arms around his waist.
2. Create a fist with the thumb side pressed against the victim's abdomen—above the navel, but below the ribcage.
3. Grab the fist with your other hand and abruptly pull upward and inward to create air pressure in the lungs

to expel the object from the windpipe (be careful not to press on the ribcage).

If the person is unconscious (or if you can't reach around him), place him on his back and straddle him, facing his head. With your other arm, push your grasped fist upward and inward into the abdomen, above the naval, but below the ribcage.

8. (True/False) A recommended cure for frostbite is to rub the affected area with snow.

9. (True/False) If you suspect that you swallowed something poisonous, you should immediately take ipecac syrup (or anything to induce vomiting).

10. How can you best survive a poisonous snake bite?

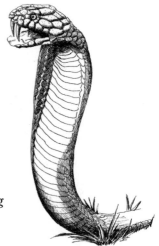

a. Using a razor blade, cut a small slit in your skin between the bite marks and suck out blood and the snake's poison. Then seek medical attention.

b. Remove restrictive clothing and jewelry and keep the bitten limb below heart level. Avoid anything that gets the heart pumping too fast, then seek medical attention.

→ FIRST AID FOR SPRAINS

A sprain is an extended stretch or tear of a ligament that connects bones. A break, on the other hand, is an actual fracture of one of the bones. The most common sprains occur in your ankles, knees, or wrists. The last thing you want to do is pretend the injury didn't happen, or move the affected area and apply heat! In contrast, remember the RICE method:

- **R** = Rest. You don't want to injure yourself anymore than you already have, so immediately rest the sprained area. Don't apply weight or move the sprained region excessively. If your ankle is sprained, use crutches to keep the weight off.
- **I** = Ice. Basically, you want to use cold therapy to reduce the inevitable swelling, to reduce blood flow to that area, and to lessen pain. Apply an ice pack, bag of ice, etc., to the sprained area for 15 minutes at a time, 4 times a day, for 48 hours. To prevent skin injury, wrap an ice bag in cloth before applying to the strain.
- **C** = Compression. Compressing the sprained area helps offer additional support and minimizes swelling. Firmly—but not too tightly—wrap an elastic bandage around the injured area.
- **E** = Elevation. Elevating the sprained area (above your heart) helps to reduce swelling and directs blood away from the affected area. If you have a sprained arm or ankle, lie down and prop the injured body part up with pillows.

To help diminish pain and reduce swelling further, you may want to take an anti-inflammatory pain medication. Some of the more common are ibuprofen (Advil, Motrin IB) and naproxen (Aleve or Naprosyn).

THE ANSWER KEY

1. ♭. Benadryl

   It's an antihistamine that can help to relieve itching. If you start coughing or experience shortness of breath, hives, or swelling around the sting, then seek medical attention immediately—you may be having an allergic reaction.

2. ♭. 10

   Just what is tetanus, and why get a shot? According to the National Institutes of Health, tetanus is a bacterium that lives in soil, saliva, dust, and manure. The bacteria usually enter the body through a deep cut, like those you might get from cutting yourself with a knife or stepping on a nail. The tetanus infection causes a painful tightening of your muscles, and can lead to lockjaw, making it impossible to open your mouth.

3. False

   Try not to break a blister unless it is too painful, or interferes with walking or working with your hands. To protect blisters—or in case they puncture—cover them with adhesive bandages or gauze pads.

4. ♭. Run cool water over the burn

5. False

If the person is still on fire, by all means smother the flames with a blanket, your jacket, or a towel, etc. DO call 911 immediately, but DON'T attempt to remove any scorched clothing directly near the burns as you could do more damage than good. Swelling will likely occur, so remove any jewelry and tight clothing near the burned area.

6. ♭. A regular-sized aspirin

Heart attacks occur when an artery that supplies oxygen to your heart becomes blocked. Aspirin acts as a blood thinner, which helps to reduce clotting, allowing more blood to flow through a blocked artery.

7. *a.* Clean the wound with cool water and a mild soap, apply a thin layer of antibiotic cream, cover with a bandage.

Avoid the use of iodine or hydrogen peroxide as they can harm tissue.

8. False

The best treatment is to re-warm the affected area. Immerse the frostbitten areas in warm (but not hot) water, or wrap the frostbitten areas in a warm blanket. Avoid using space heaters, heating pads, open flames, heat lamps, and stoves as they can cause burns, compounding the problems.

9. False

Unless you've been instructed by a reputable Poison Control Center to induce vomiting, don't take anything, as strong poisons may do a great deal of damage on the way up.

10. ♭. Remove restrictive clothing and jewelry and keep the bitten limb below heart level. Avoid anything that gets the heart pumping too fast, then seek medical attention.

32

PERSONAL HEALTH

Health is not valued till sickness comes.

—THOMAS FULLER

1. The leading cause of death in the United States is

   a. Motor vehicle accidents

   b. Firearms

   c. Cancer

   d. Major cardiovascular diseases

   e. Influenza and pneumonia

2. The accepted healthy range for a person's total cholesterol level is

   a. Less than 200 mg/dL

   b. 200–239 mg/dL

   c. 240–280 mg/dL

|||||||||||||||||||||||||||||||||||||||||||||||||||||||||||||||||||||||||||||||||||||||||||||||||||||||||||||||||||||||||||

HOW CAN YOU REGULATE YOUR CHOLESTEROL LEVELS?

- Eat less saturated fats (animal fats, dairy products) and avoid trans fats.
- If overweight, get back to your ideal weight.
- Eat more soluble fiber (whole grains, beans, fruits, vegetables).
- Quit smoking!
- Exercise on a regular basis.

|||||||||||||||||||||||||||||||||||||||||||||||||||||||||||||||||||||||||||||||||||||||||||||||||||||||||||||||||||||||||||

3. The accepted normal blood pressure is

    a. 100/40 mm Hg

    b. 120/80 mm Hg

    c. 130/80 mm Hg

    d. 140/90 mm Hg

4. On average, smokers take ____ years off their lives.

    a. 1–2

    b. 3–6

    c. 10

    d. 15

5. Which of the following hazardous substances are found in cigarette smoke?

a. Nicotine

b. Tar

c. Carbon monoxide

d. Formaldehyde

e. Ammonia

f. Hydrogen cyanide

g. Arsenic

h. DDT

i. All of the above

6. A PSA test checks for cancer of the ____.

a. Liver

b. Prostate

c. Lungs

d. Pulmonary arteries

7. Which of the following are not risks associated with being overweight?

a. Hypertension (high blood pressure)

b. Osteoarthritis (a degeneration of cartilage and its underlying bone within a joint)

c. Type 2 diabetes

d. Coronary heart disease

e. Stroke

f. Hair loss

g. Some cancers (endometrial, breast, and colon)

THE ANSWER KEY

1. *d.* Major cardiovascular diseases

Next time you feel like wolfing down a double cheeseburger, you might want to remember that cardiovascular disease (heart and vascular) is the leading cause of death in this country. There are some high risk factors beyond your control including family history, older age, and, yes—even the fact that you're a man. However, many risk factors are within your control, like whether you smoke (not a good idea), have high "bad" and low "good" cholesterol, have uncontrolled high blood pressure, are overweight, and experience lots of stress.

2. *a.* Less than 200 mg/dL

When you have too much cholesterol, you increase your risk for a heart attack or stroke.

3. *b.* 120/80 mm Hg

Blood pressure is simply the force of your blood pushing against your arteries. Having blood pressure that's too high (hypertension) can lead to many medical problems, including heart attacks, kidney failure, and strokes. High blood pressure is known as "the silent killer," as there are usually no symptoms.

4. *c*. 10

However, quitting the nasty habit at any time helps to add back some of the potentially lost years. Smokers who quit before 30 have the same life expectancy as a non-smoker.

5. i. All of the above

Not only does cigarette smoke contain the nasty chemicals listed above, but there are over 4,000 more. Of these, 43 are known carcinogens (cancer-causing agents) and 400 others are toxins.

6. b. Prostate

Only men have a prostate—a gland about the size of a walnut, situated below your bladder. Its task is to produce and release a fluid that transports your sperm during an ejaculation.

7. f. Hair loss

Generally, losing your hair is not a peril of being overweight, but you should definitely be concerned about each of the other risks—as they are pretty serious!

FITNESS

Lack of activity destroys the good condition of every human being, while movement and methodical physical exercise save it and preserve it.

— PLATO

Why should you be concerned about being physically fit? Isn't it good enough to just not be overweight? Well, clearly being overweight carries health risks, but as you'll see—the benefits of being fit go quite a bit farther.

1. Physical fitness experts generally agree that the minimum amount of *vigorous* exercise required for maintaining good cardiovascular health for those 18 and older is
   a. 50 minutes, 2 times per week
   b. 20 minutes, 3 times per week
   c. 1 hour, 5 times per week

2. Which of the following are benefits associated with cardiovascular and weight-bearing exercise?
   a. Reduced risk of heart disease and stroke
   b. Improved blood cholesterol and triglyceride levels

c. Lower blood pressure

d. Reduced risk of osteoporosis

e. Improved muscle mass

f. All of the above

3. Which of the following are benefits of strength training?

a. Increase in muscle size and tone

b. Increased muscle strength

c. Increases in tendon, bone, and ligament strength

d. All of the above

→ THE FIVE ELEMENTS OF FITNESS

Muscular Strength is simply the greatest amount of force a muscle (or group of muscles) can exert for a short duration—usually a single effort like lifting a heavy object. You don't have to be a professional weight lifter to be concerned with muscular strength. Your muscle strength determines how well you can perform your daily tasks such as yard work, household chores, carrying groceries or a child, or perhaps moving heavy objects like furniture. Building stronger muscles also makes you less susceptible to injuries.

Muscular Endurance refers to the ability of a muscle to perform repeated contractions for a period of time. For example, how many push-ups can you perform in one try? Muscular endurance is especially important for repetition of any physical activity like shoveling dirt, lifting boxes, painting, etc. Excellent muscular endurance is also critically important in almost every sport, e.g., tennis, soccer, football, swimming, and golf.

Cardiorespiratory Endurance refers to the ability of your heart, lungs, and blood to deliver oxygen and nutrients to your body tissues over prolonged periods of time. Cardiovascular fitness is usually associated with activities that elevate your pulse to 60–80% of your maximum heart rate. Some examples would be vigorous sports like basketball, hockey, soccer, swimming, and/or health club machines like treadmills, stair climbers, and stationary bicycles.

Flexibility is the ability to move muscles and joints through the limits of their range of motion. Greater flexibility leads to strengthened joints, a wider range of motion, improved posture, better muscle coordination, and reduced back pain. Flexibility can be maximized through stretching exercises and organized workout routines like Pilates and yoga. Stretching exercises should always be performed before and after every workout.

Body Composition is the ratio of lean body mass (bone, muscle, water, and internal organs) to fat. According to The National Institutes of Health, a healthy adult male should have between 8–17% of his body composed of fat. Clearly, too much fat means you're not at your optimum fitness level—and it's time to start a weight-reduction program. A simple way to measure your body fat is by your body mass index (BMI).

Multiply your weight (in lbs.) by 705 and then divide by your height in inches—twice. For example, let's say you're 5'10" tall (70 inches) and weigh 160 lbs. Multiply 160 x 705 = 112,800. Divide that number by your height, twice: 112,800/70 = 1,611; 1,611/70=23. That (23) is your body mass index.

Adults (20 and older) with a BMI between 25 and 29.9 are considered to be overweight. Those with a BMI of 30 or more are obese. (Note: if you're younger than 20, determine your BMI with the calculator tool at http://apps.nccd.cdc.gov/dnpabmi/Calculator.aspx.)

4. Working on your deltoids means that you are trying to strengthen your
   a. Upper arms
   b. Lower arms
   c. Shoulders
   d. Back

5. To reduce the risk of chronic disease in adulthood, you should engage in at least ____ minutes of *moderate* intensity physical activity (e.g., hiking, dancing, bicycling), above usual activity on most days of the week.
   a. 10
   b. 15
   c. 30
   d. 60

6. A bench press exercise strengthens which muscles?
   a. Lower arms
   b. Chest
   c. Calves
   d. Back

7. While performing weight exercises, you should

    a. Hold your breath while performing the exercise, then breathe afterwards.

    b. Breathe in while compressing the muscle, and breathe out while relaxing the muscle

    c. Breathe out while compressing the muscle, and breathe in while relaxing the muscle

8. What's an effective exercise for building your thigh (upper leg) muscles?

    a. Barbell squat

    b. Dumbbell row

    c. Upright row

    d. Dumbbell bench press

    e. All of the above

9. The guy next to you in the gym says he's going to do some curls. Which muscle is he about to start working on?

    a. Lower back

    b. Calves

    c. Biceps

    d. Neck

10. The triceps muscle is located where?

   a. Muscles on either side of the chest

   b. Calves

   c. Abdomen

   d. Back of the upper arms

11. An effective exercise for building your stomach muscles is the

   a. Abdominal crunch

   b. Stomach lunge

   c. Twisted sister

   d. Abdominal split

12. A dumbbell row is

   a. A group of stupid people lined up in a row

   b. An exercise to build your back and shoulder muscles

   c. A term for the rack of dumbbells used in weight lifting

   d. An exercise to build your neck and wrist muscles

13. (True/False) Swimming is an excellent way to lose weight.

14. (True/False) To get the most out of any workout, you really have to "work up a sweat."

15. (True/False) When it comes to working out, no pain, no gain!

THE ANSWER KEY

1. *b*. 20 minutes, 3 times per week

2. *f*. All of the above

3. *d*. All of the above
Another benefit is that you'll look better with an improved physique—helping you to increase self-esteem and confidence!

4. *c*. Shoulders
The deltoid muscles make up the rounded part of your shoulders. The deltoids' main purpose is to lift the upper arm, but they're also involved with all movements and rotations of the upper arm. To build the deltoid muscles perform military presses or lateral raise exercises.

5. *c*. 30

6. *b*. Chest

7. *c*. Breathe out while compressing the muscle, and breathe in while relaxing the muscle
Proper breathing is important during exercise, helping you to be both more efficient and more stable during your routine. Forget holding your breath, as you're likely to simply turn red, lose your energy,

and mess up your exercise. Instead, breathe out when your muscles contract (doing the work), and inhale when you relax (returning to the starting position).

8. *a.* Barbell squat

9. *c.* Biceps
The term "curls" is an abbreviation for "bicep curls"—an exercise that strengthens the upper arms.

10. *d.* Back of the upper arms

11. *a.* Abdominal crunch

12. *b.* An exercise to build your back and shoulder muscles

13. False
While swimming can be an excellent cardiovascular exercise that will tone your muscles, don't count on losing too much weight. The buoyancy of the water lessens the effort required to move you forward (unlike running, for example)—and therefore you burn fewer calories.

14. False
Sweating is your body's way of cooling itself, and is not necessarily related to the amount of exertion.

15. False

While it's common to experience soreness and/or pain a day or so after your workout, if you're feeling pain during your exercise routine, stop or you may risk injury.

SEX AND BIRTH CONTROL

1. (True/False) It's possible to contract HIV through oral sex.

2. Condoms are approximately ____% effective at preventing pregnancy.
   a. 84–98
   b. 100
   c. 75–83
   d. 40–74

3. (True/False) A woman cannot get pregnant while she is having her menstrual period.

4. Which of the following birth control methods are 100% effective at preventing an unwanted pregnancy?
   a. Early withdrawal
   b. Implant or injection
   c. Abstinence
   d. Contraceptive sponge and male spermicide
   e. Oral contraceptives, e.g., "The Pill"
   f. Diaphragm, cervical cap, and intrauterine device

5. (True/False) Condoms are 100% effective in preventing STDs.

THE ANSWER KEY

1. True

   While it's less common to transmit HIV than in other modes of trans-mission, it is indeed possible to contract it through oral sex.

2. *a*. 84–98

   Regardless of what many prophylactic companies would lead us to believe, condoms are not totally effective at preventing pregnancy. In other words, a baby is still a possibility with a condom—despite your best intentions—which helps to explain why approximately half of all pregnancies are unplanned.

3. False

   Be aware as well that sperm can live for up to five days in a woman's body.

4. *c*. Abstinence

   Yes, abstinence is the only 100% effective birth-control method. All other techniques fall short, exposing you to an unplanned pregnancy. Here are the failure rates of some common contraceptive methods:

   - *Early withdrawal = 26%*
   - *Implants and injections = 2–4%*
   - *Contraceptive sponge = 16–32%*
   - *Oral contraceptives ("The Pill") = 9%*

- *Intrauterine device (IUD) = 1%*
- *Diaphragm and cervical cap = 13%*
- *Male spermicides = 28%*

5. False

While condoms may be the only form of birth control that can help protect from STDs, there is no guarantee against being infected with (or spreading) an STD when you use them.

ALCOHOL

That's all drugs and alcohol do, they cut off your emotions in the end.

— RINGO STARR

1. In the United States, approximately how many college students die annually due to alcohol-related, unintentional injuries?

   a. 25

   b. 75

   c. 350

   d. 1,800

2. For those who drink alcohol, federal guidelines for moderation are defined as consuming ____.

   a. No drinks daily for either women or men

   b. Up to 1 drink per day for women and up to 2 drinks per day for men

   c. Up to 2 drinks per day for women and up to 3 drinks per day for men

   d. Up to 3 drinks per day for women and up to 4 drinks per day for men

3. Which of the following scenarios will make you more impaired?

a. Drinking 4 beers over 5 hours

b. Drinking 2 beers in 1 hour

c. Both about the same

4. (True/False) Switching types of alcoholic drinks—wine, beer, cocktails—makes you more drunk than sticking with one type.

5. In every state, you're considered to be "Driving Under the Influence" if your blood alcohol level (BAC) is ____ or higher.

a. .04

b. .08

c. .10

d. .20

6. (True/False) If you've had too much to drink, you can sober up by drinking coffee or caffeinated energy drinks—or taking a cold shower.

7. Which beverage has the highest alcohol content?

a. 12-oz. bottle or can of regular beer

b. 4-oz. glass of wine

c. Typical cocktail drink

d. They all have about the same.

8. (True/False) Everyone reacts differently to alcohol.

9. (True/False) If you want to stay sober, eat a large meal before you start drinking.

THE ANSWER KEY

1. *d.* 1,800

The same study concludes that almost 600,000 people each year sustain an unintentional injury while under the influence of alcohol.

2. *b.* Up to 1 drink per day for women and up to 2 drinks per day for men

3. *b.* Drinking 2 beers in 1 hour

How intoxicated you become is based on the amount you drink over time. Your body eliminates about 1 drink (beer, wine, cocktail, etc.) about every 1.5 hours. To approximate your blood alcohol level (BAC), check out online sources like http://www.bloodalcoholcalculator.org/. There are also free apps that you can download for your smart phones as well.

4. False

Mixing the types of alcohol you drink may upset your stomach, but the amount of alcohol you consume is the only factor regarding how intoxicated you will become.

5. *b.* .08

Be aware, though, that many states can declare you impaired even if you're BAC is below .08, based on a police officer's observations and/ or onsite impairment tests.

6. False

The only thing that can eliminate alcohol from your body is time. Coffee (or caffeinated energy drinks) may make you more of a "wide awake" drunk—but nothing more.

7. d. They are all about the same.

8. True

Here are a few of the variables that affect the way people react to alcohol:

- *Body weight and/or fitness level*
- *Age*
- *Gender*
- *Your mental state*
- *Tolerance*
- *Race or ethnicity*
- *Amount of food eaten right before drinking*
- *How fast you drank the alcohol*
- *If you're on prescription drugs or over-the-counter medicines*
- *Family history of alcohol problems and dependency*

9. False

Eating a large meal before you start drinking will only delay the absorption of alcohol—but will in no way diminish or stop it.

DRUGS

The basic thing nobody asks is why do people take drugs of any sort? Why do we have these accessories to normal living to live? I mean, is there something wrong with society that's making us so pressurized, that we cannot live without guarding ourselves against it?

—JOHN LENNON

What *is* a drug? The Medical Dictionary at TheFreeDictionary.com defines drug as "a chemical substance that affects the processes of the mind or body." Clearly, this encompasses many things, including substances that you might not *think* contain drugs, such as different types of foods, beverages, and even candy. Regardless of the origin— if it affects the processes of the mind or body, then it's a drug.

1. (True/False) Marijuana is essentially a harmless drug that is safe to use in moderation.

2. Which of the following is associated with cocaine use?

   a. Heart attack

   b. Paranoid psychosis

   c. Auditory hallucinations

   d. Stroke

   e. Increased blood pressure

   f. All of the above

3. (True/False) Because prescription drugs are prescribed by a doctor, they are much safer than "street" drugs.

→ THE WORLD'S MOST POPULAR DRUG

While many people assume alcohol is the most popular drug, it actually falls in second place. The world's most popular drug? Caffeine. As it is a stimulant, caffeine may initially give you the feeling that you're more alert or "awake." Beware though, as you may experience the opposite as the drug wears off. Although usually considered safe in small doses, caffeine can be mildly habit-forming. Larger doses of caffeine can cause anxiety, sleeplessness, high blood pressure, rapid heartbeat, and irritability.

4. MDMA (Ecstasy), GHB, Rohypnol, LSD, and ketamine are known as ____ drugs.

   a. Dance

   b. Club

c. Secure

d. Excitement

e. Safe

5. Marijuana is used by about _____ of 12th graders in the United States.

a. 71%

b. 5%

c. 92%

d. 21%

6. The relapse rate for those addicted to methamphetamine is about

a. 92%

b. 5%

c. 35%

d. 9%

7. (True/False) Each year, more teens enter drug rehabilitation treatment for marijuana than all other drugs combined.

THE ANSWER KEY

1. False

Marijuana use can lead to mental health problems like anxiety, depression, and panic attacks. It also impairs good judgment, perhaps altering your decisions regarding important life decisions.

2. *f.* All of the above

3. False

The reason that most of these drugs require a prescription in the first place is that they can be very dangerous and, oftentimes, quite addictive.

4. *b.* Club

These drugs are commonly known as club drugs because of their popularity at all-night dance parties known as raves. Many of these drugs are homemade by illegitimate sources, so there's no way to estimate their strength, purity, or even what other substances they may contain.

5. *d.* 21%

Contrary to what may be the popular belief—which seems to be personified in movies, television shows, and music videos—most teens don't use, and never will use, marijuana.

6. *a.* 92%

Put it another way—only about 8 out of 100 meth addicts will permanently leave the drug. Not very good odds!

7. True

ADDITIONAL RESOURCES

MANNERS AND ETIQUETTE

Dude, That's Rude!: (Get Some Manners) (Laugh And Learn) by Pamela
   Espeland and Elizabeth Verdick

*Emily Post's The Etiquette Advantage in Business: Personal Skills for
   Professional Success, Second Edition* by Peggy Post and Peter Post

*What Women Wish You Knew about Dating: A Single Guy's Guide to
   Romantic Relationships* by Stephen Simpson

WEB RESOURCES

http://www.mannersinternational.com

CAREER AND EMPLOYMENT

Instant Interviews: 101 Ways to Get the Best Job of Your Life by Jeffrey G. Allen

Negotiating Your Salary: How To Make $1000 a Minute by Jack Chapman

Resumes for Dummies by Joyce Lain Kennedy

WEB RESOURCES

http://www.jobinterviewquestions.org

http://www.Resume-Resource.com

HOME RENTING AND BUYING

Tips and Traps When Buying a Home by Robert Irwin

FINANCE AND NEGOTIATION

The 12 Investment Myths: Why Individual Investors Are Failing Miserably and How You Can Avoid Being One of Them by Jack Calhoun Jr.

The Insider's Guide to Buying a New or Used Car by Burke Leon and Stephanie Leon

Secrets of Power Negotiating by Roger Dawson

The Total Money Makeover: A Proven Plan for Financial Fitness by Dave Ramsey

WEB RESOURCES

http://www.equifax.com

http://www.fool.com

http://www.how-to-negotiate.com

TRANSPORTATION

Clueless About Cars: An Easy Guide to Car Maintenance and Repair by Lisa Christensen

Fodor's 1,001 Smart Travel Tips, 2nd Edition: Advice from the Writers, Editors & Traveling Readers at Fodor's by Fodor's

URBAN AND OUTDOOR SURVIVAL

Outdoor Survival Skills by Larry Dean Olsen and Robert Redford

Ragnar's Urban Survival: A Hard-Times Guide to Staying Alive in the City by Ragnar Benson

WEB RESOURCES

http://www.wilderness-survival.net

DOMESTIC SKILLS

Esquire The Handbook of Style: A Man's Guide to Looking Good by the Editors of *Esquire Magazine*

WEB RESOURCES

http://www.foodsafety.gov

HOME MAINTENANCE

Home Maintenance for Dummies by James Carey and Morris Carey

How Your House Works: A Visual Guide to Understanding & Maintaining Your Home by Charlie Wing

HEALTH, NUTRITION, AND LIFESTYLE

American Medical Association Handbook of First Aid and Emergency Care
  by American Medical Association

*Buzzed: The Straight Facts About the Most Used and Abused Drugs from
  Alcohol to Ecstasy, Third Edition* by Cynthia Kuhn, Scott Swartzwelder,
  and Wilkie Wilson

Complete Idiot's Guide to Total Nutrition, Fourth Edition by Joy Bauer

Men's Health Home Workout Bible by Lou Schuler and Michael Mejia

WEB RESOURCES

http://www.askmen.com

http://www.mensfitness.com

http://www.nutrition.gov

http://www.webmd.com

ABOUT THE AUTHOR

Robert Dodenhoff is a devoted single father committed to raising his own boys (Alex, 12, Brett, 15, and Conner, 17) to be independent, self-confident, and successful men. As an accomplished entrepreneur, Dodenhoff spent

many years buying, operating, and selling radio stations throughout the East. He also co-founded, and later sold, CharlestonSeafood.com, a web-based company specializing in delivering fresh seafood overnight throughout the United States. In addition, he's the founder and president of a non-profit education company offering web-based advice to youths on life-critical issues. Dodenhoff is currently the owner and president of both American Drug Testing (occupational drug-testing company) and OvernightDNA (DNA testing company)—both based in Charleston, SC. Dodenhoff and his companies have appeared in print, on television, and on the Internet, including *USA TODAY*, the *Wall Street Journal*, the Food Network, the Associated Press, NPR, *PC World,* and *Network World*. Many of the activities he enjoys with his boys are backpacking, snow skiing, golf, traveling, and boating. During his spare time, he plays drums in the original/cover bands Trancefusion and Put Tudy on the Train. Dodenhoff received a business administration degree with high honors from Rochester Institute of Technology.